THE FOUNDERS ON
CITIZENSHIP AND IMMIGRATION

THE FOUNDERS ON CITIZENSHIP AND IMMIGRATION

PRINCIPLES AND CHALLENGES IN AMERICA

Edward J. Erler
Thomas G. West
and John Marini

THE CLAREMONT INSTITUTE
FOR THE STUDY OF STATESMANSHIP AND POLITICAL PHILOSOPHY

ROWMAN & LITTLEFIELD PUBLISHERS, INC.
Lanham • Boulder • New York • Toronto • Plymouth, UK

ROWMAN & LITTLEFIELD PUBLISHERS, INC.

Published in the United States of America
by Rowman & Littlefield Publishers, Inc.
A wholly owned subsidary of The Rowman & Littlefield Publishing Group, Inc.
4501 Forbes Boulevard, Suite 200, Lanham, Maryland 20706
www.rowmanlittlefield.com

Estover Road
Plymouth PL6 7PY
United Kingdom

British Library Cataloguing in Publication Information Available

Library of Congress Cataloging-in-Publication Data:

Erler, Edward J.
  The founders on citizenship and immigration : principles and challenges in
America / by Edward J. Erler, Thomas G. West, John Marini.
       p. cm. — (Claremont Institute series on statesmanship and political phi-
losophy)
  ISBN-13: 978-0-7425-5854-0 (cloth : alk. paper)
  ISBN-10: 0-7425-5854-1 (cloth : alk. paper)
  ISBN-13: 978-0-7425-5855-7 (pbk. : alk. paper)
  ISBN-10: 0-7425-5855-X (pbk. : alk. paper)
  1. United States—Emigration and immigration—Government policy. 2. Illegal
aliens—United States. 3. Citizenship—United States. I. West, Thomas G.,
1945– II. Marini, John A. III. Title.
  JV6465.E75 2007
  325.73—dc22   2007001026

Printed in the United States of America

♾™ The paper used in this publication meets the minimum requirements of
American National Standard for Information Sciences—Permanence of Paper
for Printed Library Materials, ANSI/NISO Z39.48-1992

Table of Contents

PREFACE

The Founders on Citizenship and Immigration: Principles and Challenges in America is a volume in the Claremont Institute's series on Statesmanship and Political Philosophy. The series attempts to address issues of contemporary importance in terms of America's founding principles, a kind of resort to first principles. The underlying premise of the series is a belief in the continuing vitality of the founding principles.

In the Constitutional Convention of 1787, James Madison remarked that "he wished to maintain the character of liberality which had been professed in all the Constitutions & publications of America. He wished to invite foreigners of merit & republican principles among us. America," he concluded, "was indebted to emigration for her settlement & Prosperity." It was clearly understood by Madison and the rest of the framers that control over immigration was a matter of sovereign prerogative and that regime principles should dictate the prudential decisions as to the kind of immigrants—if any—that would benefit the regime. Those of "merit" would, of course, be most useful to the country and a vital component of their merit would be attachment to republican principles and the capacity to live an active life in accordance with those principles. The current debate about immigration is vitiated by the fact that our policymakers no longer believe that there are regime principles or that questions of merit and character have anything to do with immigration.

Ever since the Progressives advocated racially based immigration policies—claiming to have discovered scientifically provable superiorities and inferiorities among races—any attempt to introduce the issue of character or merit into the immigration debate has been dismissed as racist. The Progressives were wrong in their advocacy of race-based policies and their theories have been discredited. But the Progressive legacy lives on, making genuine debate about immigration issues almost impossible. The issue of the character of potential citizens is not a racial issue; it is a regime issue. Character—the capacity to live a life befitting republican citizens—is, as Madison indicated, crucial to the debate about immigration. This volume seeks to revive the issue of republican character in the current immigration debate and to elucidate the constitutional foundations of American citizenship.

Edward J. Erler
Series Editor

Chapter 1

INTRODUCTION:
POLITICS AND IMMIGRATION

Edward J. Erler

Immigration policy has almost always been an inside–the–beltway affair, where special interests make their pleas to an ever–compliant Congress. Public opinion has rarely played a significant role in the formulation of immigration policy—there is no special interest constituency for restricting immigration. The constituencies seeking to increase immigration—including illegal immigration—abound. Immigrant rights groups, business interests, labor unions and various ethnic advocacy groups all have a stake in the debate, hoping to magnify and extend the reach of their power by increasing immigration. Indeed, the administrative state itself has an interest in increasing immigration—especially immigrants from third–world and other undeveloped nations. These immigrants—legal and illegal—become malleable clients for the ministrations of the welfare state.

Public opinion has long opposed large–scale immigration, especially illegal immigration. One scholar opines that "it seems probable that at no time in American history has a majority of Americans favored the expansion of immigration."[1] Until recent years, however, public opinion was never

1. Samuel P. Huntington, *Who Are We? The Challenges to America's*

1

a significant factor in determining immigration policies. Both Democrats and Republicans have tolerated and even encouraged illegal immigration. Republicans sought to create a pool of cheap and exploitable labor whereas Democrats wanted a pool of future voters and a permanent underclass to serve as clients for the administrative state. For years both parties have been careful not to allow illegal immigration to become a national political issue. Republicans and Democrats were content with allowing immigration policy to be determined by special interest brokering. The public seemingly had no stake in this debate. The public might be dissatisfied with the outcome, but as long as immigration never became a political issue, public opinion would remain impotent.

The politics of immigration seem to be changing dramatically, however. On the eve of the mid–term elections of 2006, both parties were scrambling to meet public concerns. Even President George W. Bush, who favors amnesty for illegal aliens and an increase in immigration, was forced by large majorities in both houses of Congress to support a measure for constructing a security fence along part of the Mexican border, although little–noticed subsequent legislation has made it unlikely that a border fence will ever be built.[2] Against the President's wishes, and the wishes of many in both political parties, border security and public concern about illegal immigration have come to the political

---

National Identity (New York: Simon & Schuster, 2004), 329.

2. Spencer S. Hsu, "In Border Fence's Path, Congressional Roadblocks," *Washington Post*, Oct. 6, 2006, A1. "Shortly before recessing late Friday [Oct. 6], the House and Senate gave the Bush administration leeway to distribute the money to a combination of projects—not just the physical barrier along the southern border...GOP strategists [calculate] that voters do not mind the details, and that key players—including the administration, local leaders and the Mexican government—oppose a fence–only approach."

forefront. Polls from late September 2006 indicate that several House races may be decided on the issue of illegal immigration. It seems that public opinion has mounted a spirited attack against the formidable beltway defenses of the pro–immigration lobby, and it is likely that immigration policy will not easily again become an exclusive inside-the–beltway affair. But is the nation prepared for an open and honest public debate on immigration?

BORDER SECURITY, ILLEGAL IMMIGRATION AND AMNESTY

President Bush favors amnesty for illegal aliens and would probably have succeeded in achieving that goal in early 2002 had not the events of 9/11 intervened. The Bush administration, however, denies that any kind of amnesty is at work in its current proposals. We are told that amnesty is "forgiveness" and that illegal immigrants will not be "forgiven." Rather, they will be fined for breaking the law and, in addition, will have to pay back taxes. The President cautions that what critics inappropriately call "amnesty" is in reality providing a "path to citizenship" for illegal immigrants, and that it will not be a gift but "earned citizenship." But, of course, the "fine" could just as easily be called an "administrative fee," a "processing fee" or even an "admissions fee." No matter how it is sold, the Bush administration wants amnesty to be the centerpiece of its immigration policy.

In May 2006, the Senate passed the Comprehensive Immigration Reform Act. It provided amnesty for illegal aliens and created an extensive guest worker program. The Senate bill was a victory for the White House and stands as convincing testimony to how powerful the President can be when he is determined to make alliances with liberals. In stark contrast to the Senate bill, the House had previously passed enforcement–only legislation. The President, however, was unable to stampede the House into a compromise bill containing either amnesty or a guest worker program. The House was already feeling the heat of public opinion and the voters were in no mood for amnesty, however it was disguised. As of October 2006, compromise had become impossible—at least before the mid–term elections. In fact, Congress was able to stampede the President into publicly agreeing to support a border fence. Once the President can make the case—however implausibly—that the border is secure he will work hard to revive his plans for amnesty and a permanent guest worker program. In fact, the President has already claimed that the border has been secured by a "virtual" fence made up of unmanned drones, motion detectors and other modern gadgetry. As virtual proof that the border has been secured, the President points to the six thousand unarmed National Guard troops that he has ordered to the U.S.–Mexico border to serve—not as border guards—but as administrative support. So far the public remains skeptical of the President's claims. If the Republicans lose control of the House in the 2006 elections, the President is almost certain to get his amnesty plans through Congress since he can count on the cooperation of House Democrats and even a Republican controlled Senate.

In the meantime, the border remains unsecured, not only from illegal aliens, but from potential terrorists and other criminal elements. Mexico is either unwilling or unable to provide help in securing the border. It has vigorously protested the use of National Guard troops on the border. Mexico's foreign minister, Luis Ernesto Derbez, has threatened to sue if any member of the National Guard detains an illegal border crosser, although it is uncertain what the ground of the legal action might be. Derbez has also threatened to take the issue of a border fence to the United Nations, where presumably Mexico would ask for a UN condemnation of this act of national sovereignty. Mexico's animadversions on border security come at a time when criminal elements have turned the border area into a virtual state of nature. Drug traffickers and human smugglers operate with virtual impunity. In fact, the Mexican army frequently makes incursions into the United States while protecting drug traffickers.[3] MS 13, a notorious and violent gang originating in El Salvador, has extensive operations along the border and in the United States, where some twenty or thirty thousand gang members are engaged in various illegal enterprises. MS 13 traffics in drugs, humans and is even reported to have cooperated in smuggling terrorists into the United States.

MEXICO SUPPORTS ILLEGAL IMMIGRATION

It is said that there are currently 11-12 million illegal immigrants in the United States; this includes about 3.6 million who have overstayed their visas. The number is almost certainly too low: the real figure is probably closer to 20 million. In any case, any amnesty will include provisions for family reunification which will increase the numbers even more. The Comprehensive Immigration Reform Act also provides an amnesty provision for employers who hired illegal aliens in violation of federal laws. Robert Rector of the Heritage Foundation quite plausibly predicted that the revised Senate bill would have provided a "path to citizenship" for 60 million immigrants over the next twenty years.

---

3. "Mexican Government Incidents," Department of Homeland Security, U.S. Customs and Border Patrol, Office of Border Patrol, 2005 Fiscal Year Report, 4. ("From 1996 to present [September 30, 2005], the Office of Border Patrol Field Intelligence Center has confirmed two hundred and twenty-six confirmed incursions into the United States by Mexican government personnel.")

(The original bill, according to Rector, would have admitted 103 million.) And the figure of 60 million is based on the wholly unrealistic assumption that there will be no new illegal immigrants. But of course a large number of illegals will surely be lured to the United States by the prospects of another amnesty. The mere prospect of amnesty in the current debate has already produced an unprecedented surge of border crossers.

Mexico, of course, has a strong interest in increasing the number of illegal immigrants and it is only too willing to exploit its own citizens. Illegal immigration provides a convenient outlet for Mexico's desperately poor and malcontent. The one thing that the Mexican government steadfastly refuses to do is to take measures to improve its own economy and reform its corrupt government. It is far easier and more profitable for Mexico to export its poverty and its political discontent. Jorge Castañeda, Mexico's foreign minister from 2000–2003, wrote that the United States also has a vested interest in accepting immigrants from Mexico. The steady flow of Mexican malcontents to the United States is essential to Mexico's stability, he argues, and there is very little Americans can do about illegal immigration. "The consequences of trying to stop immigration would," Castañeda asserts, "certainly be more pernicious than any conceivable advantage." In fact, Mexican immigration is a "blessing" for Americans because it contributes to the stability of Mexico. Illegal immigration is thus the lesser of two "evils." In Castañeda's inimitable logic, an unstable regime on the border would be a far greater evil for the United States.[4]

The Mexican government actively encourages illegal immigration into the United States also because its economy depends upon the remissions of its citizens working in the

---

4. Jorge G. Castañeda, "Ferocious," *The Atlantic Monthly* (July, 1995), 76.

United States—25% of its entire workforce. Those remissions now amount to more than $20 billion per year, second only to oil exports as a revenue source. Mexico is actively engaged in American politics seeking to secure easier access for its citizens and promoting amnesty for those illegally in the United States. With the rise of dual-citizenship, the Mexican government can count on the loyalty of its dual citizens and fully expects that they will provide leverage for Mexican influence on policymakers. As one astute commentator remarks, "[t]he Mexican government has encouraged a pattern of dual citizenship, seeking with considerable success to export surplus labor to the United States, import migrant earnings, and retain the national loyalty of Mexican-born immigrants to the United States and their children."[5]

For Mexico, the stakes are high, and the powerful Mexican lobby is actively involved in promoting amnesty and protecting the interests of its citizens who are illegally in the United States. The move to gain acceptance for the matricula consular—an identification card issued to Mexican citizens living abroad—as a valid form of identification in the United States has, until recently, been very successful. In fact, the Bush administration issued orders through the Treasury Department that all financial institutions had to accept the matricula as valid identification and has even pushed for subsidized home loans for illegal immigrants. The Mexican lobby has also been very successful in promoting sanctuary cities. Most large cities in the United States forbid its employees—including the police—from reporting on the immigration status of its residents or cooperating with immigration officials. In sanctuary cities, the police may

---

5. Hugh Davis Graham, *Collision Course: The Strange Convergence of Affirmative Action and Immigration Policy in America* (Oxford: Oxford University Press, 2002), 184.

not stop or detain persons solely due to their immigration status or even inquire into their status while making routine traffic stops or misdemeanor arrests. These policies have, in effect, created safe havens for illegal immigrants, including criminal aliens. Although Congress passed two laws which were designed to stop state and local governments from enforcing sanctuary policies, these laws have been ignored.[6]

The Mexican lobby has also been active in promoting drivers' licenses for illegal immigrants as well as advocating increased welfare benefits. Welfare benefits are essential because they help subsidize the sub-standard wages that illegal immigrants command in the labor market. At the same time, however, the evidence is overwhelming that the availability of cheap and exploitable labor has suppressed the wages of American workers, particularly in entry-level positions. Young African-American workers are hardest hit by the influx of Mexican labor and this helps perpetuate the problems of the urban underclass. And all of this is accomplished by wages that in reality are subsidized by the federal government.

We often hear that illegal immigrant workers are essential to our economy, that the United States desperately needs workers to do jobs that Americans are unwilling to do. The United States economy, it is alleged, needs cheap, unskilled labor. Who would do the work in restaurants and hotels? Who would pick the crops? Who will dig footings? If Americans were to be employed at these jobs, we are told, the higher wages that they would demand would make these services unaffordable and the price of agricultural products would soar. But are these jobs that Americans will not perform? It is true that Americans will not work for substandard wages or allow themselves to be exploited. But cheap

---

6. See Edward Erler, "Sanctuary Cities," *Local Liberty* (Summer, 2005), 3:4–6.

labor delays capital improvement as expendable labor—and federally subsidized labor—in the short run is more attractive to business than capital improvement. In the long run, dependence on cheap labor is not profitable—it delays modernization of plants, facilities and farms. As a rule, American labor is better educated and more productive and higher wages are justified by greater productivity. Not many years ago, grain was harvested by great armies of agricultural workers armed with scythes. Now, the crops are harvested by giant machines which are more efficient and more cost effective. Almost all of our agricultural products can be harvested by machines and one or a few machine operators can be more productive than an army of pickers.

"OUT OF THE SHADOWS"

Supporters of amnesty often remark that it is necessary to bring illegal aliens already living in the United States "out of the shadows." This would entail a kind of public recognition that illegal aliens are crucial to the American economy and should be allowed to enter the mainstream of society. They do the necessary work that Americans are unwilling to do—hard physical labor for low wages and no benefits. Legalizing illegal aliens would therefore be a forthright and just recognition of the important role they have assumed in the American economic scheme. It is difficult, however, to believe that illegal aliens are in fact living in the shadows. In the Spring of 2006, protest marches brought forth millions of illegal aliens and their supporters demanding amnesty and a plethora of other rights usually reserved to citizens and legal residents. These demonstrations were, of course, calculated to bring pressure on Congress to pass comprehensive immigration reform—hardly the actions of the fearful cowering in the shadows.

The demonstrations, however, were undoubtedly a political miscalculation on the part of organizers and their supporters. It served only to harden public opinion against comprehensive reform, especially any reform involving amnesty. And the demonstrators were clear: they wanted amnesty and simply didn't see the necessity of denying the obvious—amnesty by any other name is still amnesty. It was an odd thing: illegal immigrants taking to the streets to demand a change in the law. Only in the world of postmodern citizenship could such a spectacle be possible— illegal aliens demanding a law to excuse and even dignify law–breaking. President Bush has frequently called upon the American people to show more "compassion for our neighbors to the south." But almost everyone realizes that compassion cannot be the basis for foreign policy or for immigration policy. Compassion is more likely to provoke contempt than gratitude, and the demonstrations were, I believe, a clear sign of contempt for American law.

But, of course, amnesty would entail more than just recognition of the fact that illegal aliens are present in the United States. Amnesty would not only begin the process of "chain migration" but would also entail a large increase in spending for federal benefit programs. A Congressional Budget Office report notes "that most of the additional spending would be for refundable tax credits, Medicaid, Social Security, Medicare, and Food Stamps." Although the CBO report argues that the increases will be "modest," the estimated cost for 2007–2016 is $48 billion.[7] Federal largess, of course, allows employers to pay sub–standard wages and, in effect, is a public subsidy for employers. The guest worker program seems to contemplate a permanent underclass of workers who will become wards of the administrative state.

---

7. "Congressional Budget Office Cost Estimate: S.2611, Comprehensive Immigration Reform Act of 2006," (August 18, 2006), 2, 7.

And the costs to state and local governments for welfare, medical and other services will be even greater.

THE REPUBLICAN PARTY AND THE HISPANIC VOTE

The Hispanic vote in American elections has been solidly Democratic for many years. Many Republican leaders have nevertheless voiced the opinion that the future of the Republican Party depends on the Hispanic vote. After all, we are told, the Hispanic population is the fastest growing demographic and the Republican Party cannot afford to ignore this fact.

In the last presidential election Bush claims that he received 44 percent of the Hispanic vote. No doubt the President believes that the Republican share of the Hispanic vote can be increased by amnesty—those who are the recipients of Republican compassion will eventually show their gratitude by becoming loyal Republicans. But the figure of 44 percent is almost certainly inaccurate. The latest voting studies indicate that the correct figure is, in all likelihood, significantly lower.[8] What is known for certain is that first-time Hispanic voters vote overwhelmingly Democratic and that after two or three generations Hispanics are still solidly entrenched in the Democratic Party. In other words, the Hispanic vote is not "in play" in any realistic sense. Republicans have had some success in attracting non-Catholic Hispanic voters, but their numbers are still relatively small, although steadily growing. In all probability Bush only received 33 percent of the Catholic Hispanic vote in 2004.[9]

---

8. David L. Leal, et al., "The Latino Vote in the 2004 Election," *PS: Political Science and Politics* (January 2005), 37:41–49; Robert Suro, Richard Fry, Jeffrey Passel, *Hispanics and the 2004 Election: Population, Electorate and Voters* (Washington, D.C.: Pew Hispanic Center, 2005), 11–15.
9. *Hispanics and the 2004 Election*, 14.

Many in the Republican Party believe that Republicans can beat the Democrats at their own game. But to be competitive, the Republican Party will have to become more like the Democratic Party; it will have to become the party of big government and the party of the welfare state. James G. Gimpel and Karen Kaufmann, political scientists at the University of Maryland, argue that "Republican aversion to 'big government' solutions will continue to plague Republican efforts at Latino recruitment. One must ask whether Republicans are really willing to change their traditional stands on health care and social welfare programs in order to compete for this constituency. An alliance on cultural issues may create opportunities for enhanced Latino enrollment, but only if these concerns displace social welfare issues in their importance to Hispanic voters." Thus, these two analysts conclude, "[t]he GOP is in no position to make the kind of policy promises that would be required to bring Latinos over to the Republican side, much less deliver on such promises...And one must not overlook the fact that Republicans pay significant opportunity costs in chasing after the Latino vote. Their time may be better spent on trying to close the gender gap or attracting the loyalties of white working–class voters who have regularly shown an independent streak."[10]

It seems, however, that President Bush's agenda of "compassionate conservatism" has in fact become big government conservatism. If the Republicans have consciously made the choice to compete with the Democrats on their own grounds, the welfare state will have no organized political opposition.

---

10. James G. Gimpel and Karen Kaufmann, "Impossible Dream or Distant Reality? Republican Efforts to Attract Latino Voters," Center for Immigration Studies (August, 2001), 8.

Immigration and the Administrative State

Immigrants have been co-opted by the administrative state in great numbers and they show their gratitude by remaining loyal Democrats. Even "compassionate conservatism" is unlikely to break the Democratic stranglehold on the Hispanic vote. Increased immigration—and a quick and smooth path to citizenship—will help the Democratic Party, not the Republicans. The Comprehensive Immigration bill favored by the President will go a long way to transforming the Republican Party—but the most likely outcome is that all the political benefits will result to the Democrats. Senator Kennedy and the Democratic Party got the best of the bargain in the Immigration Reform and Control Act of 1986 and they will get the best of the bargain in 2006 if comprehensive immigration reform is passed.

One important aspect of immigration policy that is conspicuously absent from the current debate is whether immigrants should be expected to adapt to an American way of life, including exclusive allegiance to the Constitution and its principles. Of course, the minions of the administrative state wish to have immigrants fill the ranks of dependent classes who need the ministrations of the welfare state. The Immigration Act of 1965 was understood by its architects to be a kind of affirmative action remedy for what were deemed racist exclusionary policies of past immigration legislation. Previous immigration laws had been based on national origins and attempted to perpetuate the racial and ethnic mix already in existence in the country. The emphasis was on allowing immigrants to enter who would have the least trouble adapting to the American way of life because their social norms and cultural imperatives were not essentially different—or at least similar enough—to make adaptation relatively easy. This adaptation would entail, above all, acquiring allegiance to the American constitutional system and its attendant rule of law.

Theodore White lamented some years ago that "the Immigration Act of 1965 changed all previous patterns, and in so doing, probably changed the future of America...The new act of 1965 was noble, revolutionary—and probably the most thoughtless of the many acts of the Great Society."[11] Oddly enough, President Lyndon Johnson, who signed the legislation on October 3, 1965, insisted that "[t]his bill is not a revolutionary bill." Johnson, of course, always described his own achievements in grandiose terms and it is more than a little surprising to find him underplaying the importance of legislation for which he was responsible. "It will not reshape the structure of our daily lives," the President reassured the nation, "or really add importantly to our wealth or our power. Yet it is still one of the most important acts of this Congress and of this administration. For it does repair a very deep and painful flaw in the fabric of American justice. It corrects a cruel and enduring wrong in the conduct of the American nation. " One perceptive commentator has noted that "[t]he bill, in fact, changed the whole course of American immigration history, although it did so along lines that were already apparent for the few who had eyes to see. In addition, it facilitated a great increase in the volume of immigration....The most striking effect of the new law has been further to increase the share of immigration slots going to Asia and Latin America."[12]

The result of the 1965 act was a massive increase in immigration from Third World countries. Great numbers came to the United States, both legally and illegally, driven by

---

11. Theodore H. White, *America in Search of Itself* (New York: Warner Books, 1982), 363.

12. Roger Daniels, *Coming to America: A History of Immigration and Ethnicity in American Life*, 2nd ed. (New York: Harper Collins, 2002), 341.

the immense pressures of despotism and economic depriva-
tion in their native countries. The stated purpose of the act
was to "correct a cruel and enduring wrong" in America's
immigration policies; the unstated purpose of the act was
to change the racial and ethnic mix of the population of
the United States, not only as a compensation for past racial injustice, but also as a way of consolidating the welfare
state by adding to its list of client groups. Immigrants from
Third World countries have a more difficult time adapting
to American customs and laws and, indeed, show less willingness to do so. These immigrants are more likely to need
the services of the welfare state and the administrative state
was only too willing to specify the terms and conditions for
their adjustment to American society. In fact, the administrative state encouraged immigrants to retain their cultures
by promoting multiculturalism. The administrators—and
eventually the immigrants—demanded that America should
change to accommodate those with different cultures. The
old goal of the "melting pot" was now mocked as a racist legacy in the new universe of multiculturalism. Indeed,
demands that immigrants adapt to American habits and
manners were derided as cultural genocide, a product of
America's overweening arrogance, an arrogance fueled by
the anachronistic notion of American exceptionalism.

The welfare bureaucracy—and its allies in the "civil
rights community"—was eager to perpetuate the dependence of new immigrants, whether legal or illegal. Bilingual
education, affirmative action and other forms of welfare dependency came to the forefront. One scholar remarks that
"[t]he eligibility of 80 percent of immigrants to America
for affirmative action programs made a mockery of the historical rationale that minority preferences compensated for
past discrimination in America."[13] Furthermore, this scholar

---

13. Davis, *Collision Course*, 192

notes, "[t]he proliferation since the 1970s of bilingual/bicultural education programs in American schools has further segregated and isolated Mexican (and Hispanic) children from the American mainstream and weakened the acquisition of English literacy and competence in school subjects leading to higher education and advancement in America's high–tech economy."[14] Most scholars deny, of course, that there was any concerted effort on the part of the administrative state to co-opt newcomers. The policies were piecemeal and the consequences seemingly unintended. But, of course, the administrative state has a life of its own. It seeks to extend the reach of its influence and magnify its power and it does so largely out of sight of the public. Its weapons are administrative regulations and policies of indirection, all backed by the cooperation of a compliant court system.

The Immigration Act of 1965 fit the goals of the administrative state admirably. It was one of the three great acts of legislation, along with the Civil Rights Act of 1964 and the Voting Rights Act of 1965, which were vigorously promoted by Lyndon Johnson. All three acts sought to end racial discrimination. The administrative agencies charged with their implementation, however, quickly transformed laws ostensibly prohibiting racial discrimination into laws requiring racial discrimination—affirmative action in employment, racial set–asides and quotas in contracting and racially proportional results in voting. And courts were willing accomplices, citing the necessity of deferring to administrative expertise.[15] The Immigration Act had its niche. As one administrator remarked, "without fully realizing it, we have left the time when the nonwhite, non–Western part of

---

14. Ibid., 184, 83, 173.
15. See Edward J. Erler, "The Future of Civil Rights: Affirmative Action Redivivus," *Notre Dame Journal of Law, Ethics & Public Policy* 11 (1997), 26–33.

our population could be expected to assimilate to the dominant majority. In the future, the white Western majority will have to do some assimilation of its own."[16] The American middle classes—sometimes called the selfish classes by intellectuals and welfare state administrators—who aspire to secure a comfortable bourgeois existence and the enjoyment of the fruits of their own labor will eventually find themselves without a working majority to oppose the expansion and eventual triumph of the welfare state. The recalcitrance of this class is the last barrier to the final victory of the administrative state. If present trends continue, some time in the twenty–first century the middle classes will become politically impotent. Their anti–tax, anti–immigration and anti–big government sentiments will be overwhelmed by those who depend upon big government and the largess of the administrative state. No plan or conspiracy is necessary: the administrative state has a life of its own, with great adaptability, and with sure instincts for its own survival—it is animated by the collective will to power of the administrative class.

IMMIGRATION AND REGIME QUESTIONS: THE VIEW FROM THE FOUNDING

In the *Declaration of Independence* one piece of evidence adduced to prove that King George's purpose has been "the establishment of an absolute tyranny over these states" was the fact that "He has endeavored to prevent the population of these states; for that purpose obstructing the laws for naturalization of foreigners, refusing to pass others to

---

16. Martha Farnsworth Riche, Director of Population Studies, Population Reference Bureau, and later Director of the Bureau of the Census in the Clinton Administration, quoted in *Time Magazine*, November 18, 1993, editorial.

encourage their migrations hither, and raising the conditions of new appropriations of lands." Thus, the issue of immigration and naturalization was present at the beginning. In the *Summary View of the Rights of British America* (1774) Jefferson had argued that the natural right of expatriation was "a right, which nature has given to all men, of departing from the country in which chance, not choice has placed them."[17] Choice, of course, implies reason and the exercise of the right to expatriation depends on reasoned choice, i.e., consent. If emigration is a natural right, it must nevertheless be conceded that naturalization (despite its name) is merely a conventional right. And even the natural right to emigration must surely be exercised within the context of the existence of sovereign nations. The right to leave the country where "chance" has placed one may be a natural right, but there is no correspondent right to emigrate to any country without its consent. As the Supreme Court once rightly noted "it is an accepted maxim of international law, that every sovereign nation has the power, as inherent in sovereignty, and essential to self–preservation, to forbid the entrance of foreigners within its dominions, or to admit them only in such cases and upon such conditions as it may see fit to prescribe."[18]

In the early 1780s Jefferson once again turned his attention to the question of immigration. This time, Jefferson considered the issue in the context of conventional right rather than natural right. That is, the question of immigration as a practical matter had to be considered within the context of the sovereign right of each nation to determine its own immigration policies. In *Notes on the State of Virginia*

---

17. Jefferson, "Summary View of the Rights of British America," in *Jefferson: Writings*, Merrill Peterson, ed. (New York: Library of America, 1984), 105.
18. Nishimura Ekiu v. U.S., 142 U.S. 651, 659 (1892).

Jefferson reflected on the question of whether or not to confine population increase to native stock alone or to encourage foreign importation. "[A]re there inconveniences," Jefferson queried "to be thrown into the scale against the advantage expected from a multiplication of numbers by the importation of foreigners?" Jefferson began his answer with a reflection on regime principles:

> It is for the happiness of those united in society to harmonize as much as possible in matters which they must of necessity transact together. Every species of government has its specific principles. Ours perhaps are more peculiar than those of any other in the universe. It is a composition of the freest principles of the English constitution, with others derived from natural right and natural reason. To these nothing can be more opposed than the maxims of absolute monarchies.[19]

That every type of regime has its "peculiar" principles is a truth known to all political philosophers. America is "more peculiar" because it is the first attempt to ground a regime in practice on "natural right and natural reason." It is also important to note that not all the principles of the English constitution (and common law) were adopted by America, but only its "freest principles," i.e., those compatible with natural right and natural reason.

We learn from that great classifier of regimes, Aristotle, that citizens must have the character—or manners and habits—appropriate to each regime. The same character would not be suitable for a citizen of monarchy and of a republic. "Suppose," Jefferson queried, "20 millions of republican Americans thrown all of a sudden into France, what would be the condition of that kingdom? If it would be more turbulent, less happy, less strong, we may believe that the

---

19. *Notes on the State of Virginia,* in *Writings,* Query VIII, 211.

addition of half a million of foreigners to our present numbers would produce a similar effect here."[20] Thus the character of citizens is essential to the maintenance of regime principles. A radical change in the character of the citizens would be tantamount to a regime change just as surely as a revolution in its political principles. Thus, guarding regime principles necessarily means addressing not only issues of education but also the issue of character in immigration policy.[21]

One has only to glance at Locke's *Some Thoughts Concerning Education*, a book that was widely read and admired in America in the years leading up to the founding, to get a sense of the character suitable for republican citizens and their rulers. Industry, independence and self–government are the principal virtues that make up the republican character. In short, republican education inculcates the habits and manners of free and self–governing citizens. Two astute commentators have noted that "in Locke's view, to be free is to be self-governing. But to be self–governing is to be guided by reason....Each of us thus has a *moral* responsibility to cultivate our rational faculties and to overcome those moral failings that stand in the way of reasonableness."[22] Only a self–governing individual, that is, an individual who is capable of ruling his passions by reason or calculation, can be a member of a self–governing people. It is perfectly in this spirit that *The Federalist* remarks that only "the reason...of the public...ought to control and regulate the government. The passions ought to be controlled and regulated

---

20. Ibid., 212.
21. See Aristotle, *Politics*, 1303a21-1303b3.
22. Ruth W. Grant and Nathan Tarcov, eds., "Introduction," John Locke, *Some Thoughts Concerning Education and Of the Conduct of the Understanding* (Indianapolis: Hackett Publishing Co., 1996), xii (emphasis original).

by the government."[23] Since "the people are the only legitimate fountain of power, and it is from them that the constitutional charter, under which the several branches of government hold their power, is derived" the "reason...of the public"—and the government's power to regulate and control the passions—ultimately rests on the reason (moderation) and "vigilant and manly spirit which actuates the people of America—a spirit which nourishes freedom, and in return is nourished by it."[24]

Jefferson noted that most of the immigrants to America would be refugees from absolute monarchies, the prevailing system of nations in the eighteenth century. One would think, at first blush, that these refugees would be ideal citizens of a republic because their enthusiasm for liberty would naturally be spurred by their experiences with despotism. Jefferson, however, saw more subtle influences at work and rightly argued that the habits and manners of freedom are not so easily acquired—enthusiasm for liberty is not an adequate substitute for habituation to liberty. "They will bring with them the principles of the governments they leave, imbibed in their early youth; or, if able to throw them off, it will be in exchange for an unbounded licentiousness, passing, as is usual, from one extreme to another. It would be a miracle were they to stop precisely at the point of temperate liberty."

Immigrants arriving from despotic nations would be used to the yoke of despotism and will have developed the servile habits engendered by despotism from "their early youth." They will hardly notice small depredations upon their liberty which often serve as early warnings of open

---

23. Alexander Hamilton, James Madison, and John Jay, *The Federalist Papers*, No. 49, introduction and notes by Charles R. Kesler, Clinton Rossiter, ed. (New York: New American Library, 1999), 314.
24. Ibid., No. 57, 350; No. 14, 99; No. 40, 250.

assaults upon liberty. Those who have engendered the habits of freedom, however, are more jealous of their liberties and less likely to tolerate affronts to their liberty, whether real or merely imagined. These refugees from despotism will also not be able easily to acquire the habits of self–government. Thrust suddenly into freedom, they will be guided by passion rather than reason. The virtue of self–government requires habituation and education—it must be cultivated and rarely flourishes when conferred upon those not prepared to receive it, either by disposition or training.

Rather than taking their place easily among a self-governing people, Jefferson anticipated that those fleeing despotism will find it difficult to maintain the spirit of self–government, and in all likelihood will find themselves dissolving into a "heterogeneous, incoherent, distracted mass."[25] It is preferable from the strict republican point of view, Jefferson concluded, to populate the country from its native stock so that future citizens will begin their preparation for self-government from the moment of birth, and the love of liberty would be imbibed with their mothers' milk, becoming as it were a kind of second nature.[26]

The only exception that Jefferson admitted were "useful artificers," who should be encouraged to emigrate to America—indeed the nation should "spare no expense in obtaining them." But once they teach Americans the useful arts they should "go to the plough and the hoe" to develop the habits and manners of republican citizens. Agriculture is a stern republican schoolmaster, inculcating the habits of independence, honesty and self–reliance. Jefferson was not entirely facetious when he remarked that "[t]hose who

25. *Notes on the State of Virginia,* 215.
26. See Abraham Lincoln, "Address Before the Young Men's Lyceum of Springfield, Illinois," in *The Collected Works of Abraham Lincoln,* Roy P. Basler, ed. (New Brunswick: Rutgers University Press, 1953), I:112.

labour in the earth are the chosen people of God, if ever he had a chosen people, whose breasts he has made his peculiar deposit for substantial and genuine virtue." Most of all, farmers are independent, not even "looking up to heaven" but relying on "their own soil and industry" to secure "their subsistence." "Dependence," Jefferson argues, "begets subservience and venality" and "suffocates the germ of virtue" thus preparing the subservient to be "fit tools for the designs of ambition." If people become subservient in their character and habits, it is certain that sooner or later they will succumb to the ever–present ambitions of men who seek to reduce them to despotism. Jefferson thus concludes that "[i]t is the manners and spirit of a people which preserve a republic in vigour."[27]

Jefferson may have underestimated the power of American principles to assimilate and transform immigrants into American citizens. A commitment to common principles—those adumbrated in the Declaration of Independence—and the willingness and wherewithal to live by those principles seems to be a sufficient ground for citizenship. Those principles, as Lincoln mentioned, were "the father of all morals among us" and were the common ground of citizenship. These principles, of course, presume a self–governing, self–reliant people dedicated to the ends of free government, equal protection of equal rights within the rule of law. This was the way millions of immigrants were not only assimilated to the American way of life, but were also willing to fight and die for the principles that animated that way of life. Allegiance to regime principles was primary. Habits, manners and morals befitting free citizens would follow inevitably in due course. But the goals of the administrative state are not the goals that the Founders established, nor the goals that Lincoln perpetuated. Freedom was the goal of the

---

27. *Notes on the State of Virginia*, Query XIX, 291.

government envisioned by the Founders and this goal required limited government and a self-reliant and resourceful people. Welfare is the goal of the administrative state and dependence is the quality required of its citizens. But, of course, dependents are not really citizens—they are clients who have no aspirations for living an independent life. They are the anonymous ciphers who populate the welfare state and who have long ago forgotten—if they ever knew—that freedom was once the goal of politics.

Chapter 2

AMERICAN CITIZENSHIP AND POSTMODERN CHALLENGES

Edward J. Erler

In the past dozen years, the growing problem of illegal immigration has provoked a wide–ranging debate about the constitutional status of American citizenship. For many years it has been assumed that birthright citizenship is the ground of American citizenship and that children of illegal aliens born within the geographical limits of the United States are automatically citizens by birth. This assumption has been challenged by some scholars and legislators. In 1995 legislation was introduced in the House of Representatives seeking "to deny automatic citizenship at birth to children born in the United States to parents who are not citizens or permanent resident aliens." The legislation failed but was renewed in 1997 and subsequent years. The latest attempt, the Citizenship Reform Act of 2005, met the same fate as its predecessors, even though it had more than eighty cosponsors. Republican House leaders refused to allow the proposal to come to a floor vote.

These legislative attempts to limit the reach of birthright citizenship were inspired, in large measure, by public concern about the seemingly intractable problems of illegal immigration. By 1995 it had become increasingly evident that the enforcement provisions of the Immigration Reform and Control Act of 1986 had failed. That act, in addition to providing amnesty for nearly 3 million illegal aliens, promised increased border security and criminal penalties for employers who knowingly employed illegals. The amnesty provisions of IRCA were highly successful; the enforcement provisions were never taken seriously. But of course no one except a few naïve Republicans—including Senator Alan Simpson, cosponsor of the legislation—believed that there was any intention to enforce the employer sanctions or control the flow of illegal aliens crossing the border. In fact, as many predicted, the amnesty provisions provided a new incentive for illegal immigrants—the hope (perhaps even the expectation) that the amnesty provision of IRCA was merely the precursor to a series of ever-more generous offers.

By 1995 many had come to believe that the denial of automatic birthright citizenship for the children of illegal aliens would eliminate a powerful incentive for illegal border crossers. The public had become acutely aware of the phenomenon known as "anchor babies." The child of an illegal alien born within the geographical limits of the United States automatically receives American citizenship. This newly minted citizen immediately becomes eligible for a variety of state and federal benefits and in future years acquires "minority" status for affirmative action benefits. More importantly, however, when "anchor babies" reach twenty-one they can sponsor their parents and other family members for legal permanent residency and eventual citizenship. The populations of entire villages in Mexico have been transplanted to the United States almost intact, the "chain-migration" having begun with one anchor baby. And it is not just the economically distressed who seek the benefits of American citizenship. In 2003 the *Los Angeles Times* reported the influx of middle- and upper-class women who cross the border from Mexico with temporary visas to have children in the United States. In recent years a thriving travel industry has been created to cater to women from South Korea and Hong Kong who travel to the United States to have their babies knowing the great advantages that American citizenship will confer on their children.[1] It is difficult to imagine that the framers of the Fourteenth Amendment meant to confer citizenship upon the children of such casual sojourners. Most countries have abandoned birthright citizenship. England did so in 1981 and Ireland in 2004, the last of the original fifteen European Union nations to give up birthright citizenship. In the world of mass migrations, most countries have recognized that the idea of a sovereign nation is incompatible with birthright citizenship.

In 1995 Walter Dellinger, then Assistant Attorney General, Office of Legal Counsel, testified before a joint session of the Subcommittee on Immigration and Claims and the Subcommittee on the Constitution that the proposed legislation was patently unconstitutional. Such a drastic change in "the fundamental legal principle governing citizenship" would require a constitutional amendment, he argued. Even a constitutional amendment, Dellinger concluded, would "conflict with basic constitutional principles." While not "technically unlawful," an amendment would "flatly contradict our constitutional history and our constitutional traditions." "The fundamental legal principle governing citizenship," Dellinger asserted, "has been that birth within the territorial limits of the United States confers United States citizenship." Thus, he contended, "[t]he Constitution itself rests on this principle of the common law," and the

---

1. Anna Gorman, "Affluent Cross Border to U.S. for Childbirth," *Los Angeles Times*, April 17, 2003, B1; Barbara Demick, "The Baby Registry of Choice: Thousands of Pregnant South Koreans Travel to the U.S. to Give Birth to American Citizens," *Los Angeles Times*, May 25, 2002, A1.

Fourteenth Amendment was merely "intended to codify the common law."[2]

Similar testimony was given in 1997 by Dawn E. Johnsen, Acting Assistant Attorney General, Office of Legal Counsel, before the Subcommittee on Immigration and Claims. According to Johnsen, "the unmistakable purpose" of the Fourteenth Amendment's language that "All persons born or naturalized in the United States, and subject to the jurisdiction thereof, are citizens of the United States and of the State wherein they reside" was "to constitutionalize the existing Anglo–American common law rule of *jus soli* or citizenship by place of birth." The phrase "subject to the jurisdiction thereof" was merely "meant to reflect the existing common law exception for discrete sets of persons who were deemed subject to a foreign sovereign and immune from U.S. laws, principally children born in the United States of foreign diplomats, with the single additional exception of children of members of Indian tribes." "Apart from these extremely limited exceptions," Johnsen concluded, "there can be no question that children born in the United States of aliens are subject to the full jurisdiction of the United States."[3]

Both Johnsen and Dellinger agreed that the purpose of the Fourteenth Amendment's citizenship clause was to make *jus soli* the constitutional basis for American citizenship. For, as Dellinger remarked, "the principal alternative system, *jus sanguinis*, used in most civil law European

---

2. Hearing Before the House Subcomm. on Immigration and Claims and on the Constitution, Comm. on the Judiciary, (Dec. 13, 1995) (statement of Walter Dellinger, Assistant Attorney Gen.), available in LEXIS, Legis Library, Cngtst File.

3. Hearing Before the House Subcomm. on Immigration and Claims, Comm. on the Judiciary, (June 25, 1997) (statement of Dawn E. Johnsen, Acting Assistant Attorney Gen., Office of Legal Counsel), available in LEXIS, Legis Library, Cngtst File.

countries, grants citizenship by descent or blood—that is, according to the citizenship of one's parents. This system obviously could not have operated in the United States at its inception, where, except for American Indians, the inhabitants were citizens of other countries." Dellinger doesn't seem to recognize that this situation was not unique to the United States. It is the problem of all new nations—it is the problem of founding. When a new nation is founded, there are no citizens by birth in the newly created nation—even the Founders themselves are not "natural born" citizens of the regime they create. The simple lesson here—one that seems to escape Dellinger entirely—is that citizens are made, not born. Citizenship is conventional, not natural. Citizens do not spring from the earth as the *"geganai"*—the earth born—in Plato's *Republic*. The *geganai*, of course, have an indissoluble attachment to their political community as citizens "by nature." The question of justice that is resolved by Plato's device—how a people can ever justly claim title to a particular territory to the exclusion of others—is not easily resolved in practice, if it ever can be resolved. Virtually every nation in the world is a nation of immigrants; they have all come from someplace else, displacing the original inhabitants. The United States is not unique in this regard, no matter how much some internationalists argue that because America is a nation of immigrants it should be especially liberal in its immigration policies.

I testified before the House Committees in 1995 and 1997, taking the position that the proposed legislation was a constitutional exercise of Congress' power under section 5 of the Fourteenth Amendment. In fact, I sought to demonstrate that Congress had exercised its section 5 powers on many occasions. It was universally conceded in 1868 that the citizenship clause of the Fourteenth Amendment did not make Indians citizens because they were not "subject to the jurisdiction" of the United States. Subsequent legislation brought members of various tribes within the jurisdiction of the United States and extended offers of citizenship to those who consented. At first, Congress made offers on a tribe–by–tribe basis, eventually passing an offer to bring all native persons within the jurisdiction of the United States in 1924. Throughout my testimony, I argued that the basis for citizenship in the American regime was not the common law, but consent. The framers of the Constitution saw the common law doctrine of perpetual allegiance as a feudal legacy that had been repealed by the Declaration of Independence, I argued, and the framers of the Fourteenth Amendment explicitly took the same point of view.[4]

THE CONSTITUTION AND CITIZENSHIP

It has often been pointed out that the Constitution, while it refers to citizens, does not define citizenship. Indeed, there was no explicit definition of citizenship until the Fourteenth Amendment was ratified in 1868. Article IV of the Constitution commands that "[t]he citizens of each State shall be entitled to all Privileges and Immunities of Citizens in

---

4. Hearing Before the House Subcomm. on Immigration and Claims and on the Constitution, Comm. on the Judiciary, (Dec. 13, 1995) (statement of Professor Edward Erler), available in LEXIS, Legis Library, Cngtst File; Hearing Before the House Subcomm. on Immigration and Claims, Comm. on the Judiciary, (June 25, 1997) (statement of Professor Edward Erler), available in LEXIS, Legis Library, Cngtst File. The present article draws on my congressional testimony as well as some of my previous publications: "Immigration and Citizenship," in *Loyalty Misplaced: Misdirected Virtue and Social Disintegration,* Gerald Frost, ed. (London: The Social Affairs Unit, 1997), 71–89; "From Subjects to Citizens: The Social Compact Origins of American Citizenship," in *The American Founding and the Social Compact,* Ronald J. Pestritto and Thomas G. West, eds. (Lanham: Lexington Books, 2003), 163–197; "Citizenship," in *The Heritage Guide to the Constitution,* David Forte and Matthew Spaulding, eds. (Washington: The Heritage Foundation, 2005), 384–386.

the several States." The privileges and immunities clause unmistakably implies a general United States citizenship. Joseph Story accurately noted that "[i]t is obvious that if the citizens of each state were to be deemed aliens to each other, they could not take or hold real estate, or other privileges, except as other aliens." Story is therefore driven to the conclusion that "[t]he intention of this clause was to confer on them, as one may say, a general citizenship, and to communicate all the privileges and immunities which the citizens of the same state would be entitled to under the same circumstances."[5]

Members of the House of Representatives must be citizens of the United States for seven years to be eligible for election and Senators for nine years. Representatives and Senators can thus be naturalized citizens. The President, however, must be "a natural born Citizen, or a Citizen of the United States at the time of the Adoption of this Constitution" and "been fourteen Years a Resident within the United States." Citizenship of the United States thus clearly preexisted the adoption of the Constitution. The Declaration mentions the American people in both their political capacity and their moral capacity. Americans are "one people" and the "good People." The American people are one people—and fellow citizens—*because* they are a good people and they are a good people because they are dedicated to the principles of the Declaration, most particularly to the principle that the "just powers" of government derive their authority from "the consent of the governed." The Declaration thus proclaims itself to be the constitutive document of the American regime.

The Constitution, of course, was created by "We the people"; the Constitution did not create the people. Article

---

5. Joseph Story, *Commentaries on the Constitution of the United States* (Boston: Little, Brown and Company, 1878), 2:§187.

VII specifies that the Constitution was "Done in Convention by the Unanimous Consent of the States present the Seventeenth Day of September in the Year of our Lord one thousand seven hundred and Eighty seven and of the Independence of the United States of America the Twelfth." Thus the "Independence of the United States" is fixed on the date of the Declaration of Independence. Citizenship is also fixed in the Declaration. Citizenship was not defined in the Constitution because it had already been defined in the Declaration and the basis of citizenship was the "consent of the governed." Citizenship in the Declaration is both natural and conventional. That is, while citizenship has a basis in nature—that all men are "created equal" and thus legitimate rule must proceed from "the consent of the governed"—it is conventional in the sense that it establishes a particular regime with a particular citizenry made up only of those who accept the ends or purposes for which government was established.

No one born before the Declaration could be a "natural born" citizen. Since the minimum age for eligibility to the Presidency was thirty–five years, it was necessary to carve out an exception until at least thirty–five years after the adoption of the Declaration of Independence. Anyone who was a "Citizen of the United States" on the day the Constitution was adopted and a resident of the United States for fourteen years—i.e., since the beginning of the Revolution—would be eligible for the highest office of the land without being a natural born citizen. It was not until Martin Van Buren, the eighth president who was born in 1782, that a natural born citizen ascended to the highest elective office.

The Constitution clearly specifies two unequal classes of citizens—those natural born citizens eligible to occupy the office of the presidency and those naturalized citizens who are permanently barred from that office. The requirement that the President be a natural born citizen seems to have been uncontroversial and inspired principally by the reluctance of the framers to entrust the powers of commander in chief to a foreign born citizen.[6] Thus, the contention that "the Constitution repudiated graded citizenship as well as any notion that native-born and naturalized citizens should possess different sets of rights, and confirmed the principle that U.S. citizenship, once conferred, would be uniform and complete" is belied by the text of the Constitution.[7] The Constitution distinguishes between natural born and naturalized citizens, although it must always be kept in mind that "natural born" and "naturalized" are terms of art. Both forms of citizenship are conventional and the distinction between them is also conventional.

DID THE DECLARATION ADOPT BIRTHRIGHT CITIZENSHIP?

This complex specification of dates in the Constitution makes it abundantly clear that United States citizenship began with the Declaration of Independence and that the principles of the Declaration inform the American idea of citizenship. Ever since *Calvin's Case* (1608) Britain had relied on "birth right subjectship" or "natural ligeance" as the foundation of "citizenship." In *Calvin's Case* Sir Edward Coke argued that "natural ligeance" "originally is due by nature and birth." It is "a true and faithful obedience of the subject due to his sovereign. This ligeance and obedience is

---

6. John Jay, Letter to George Washington, July 25, 1787, in *The Records of the Federal Convention of 1787*, Max Farrand, ed. (New Haven: Yale University Press, 1966 [originally published in 1911]), 3:61.

7. Reed Ueda, "Naturalization and Citizenship," in *Harvard Encyclopedia of American Ethnic Groups*, Stephen Thernstrom, ed. (Cambridge: Harvard University Press, 1982), 736–737;

an incident inseparable to every subject: for as soon as he is born, he oweth by birth–right ligeance obedience to his sovereign."[8] On the eve of the American Revolution, William Blackstone, citing Coke as his authority, noted that

> natural allegiance is such as is due from all men born within the king's dominions immediately upon their birth [citing *Calvin's Case*]. For immediately upon their birth, they are under the king's protection...Natural allegiance is therefore a debt of gratitude; which cannot be forfeited, cancelled, or altered, by any change of time, place, or circumstance...For it is a principle of universal law, that the natural–born subject of one prince cannot by any act of his own, no, not by swearing allegiance to another, put off or discharge his natural allegiance of the former: for this natural allegiance was intrinsic, and primitive, and antecedent to the other.[9]

Although Blackstone argued that natural allegiance "is founded in reason and the nature of government," he admitted that the concept was an inheritance from the "feodal system," deriving from the "mutual trust or confidence subsisting between the lord and vassal." And "[b]y an easy analogy the term allegiance was soon brought to signify all other engagements, which are due from subjects to their prince."[10] Under the feudal regime there were, strictly speaking, no citizens. Neither Coke nor Blackstone ever refers to birthright citizenship and both describe the allegiance due to a king as involuntary and perpetual. This is the relation of master and subject in which subjects can never gain the

---

8. 2 Howell's *State Trials* 576 (1608). For an in–depth discussion of *Calvin's Case* see Edward Erler, "From Subjects to Citizens: The Social Compact Origins of American Citizenship," in *The American Founding and the Social Compact*, 170–178.

9. William Blackstone, *Commentaries on the Laws of England*, (Oxford: Clarendon Press, 1765–1769 [reprinted by University of Chicago Press, 1979]), 1:357–358.

10. Ibid., 1:354–355.

elevated status of citizens who freely accept obligations and have the obligation to assert rights. James Wilson almost certainly had Blackstone in mind when in 1793 he famously noted that "[u]nder the Constitution of the United States there are citizens, but no subjects."[11] Wilson, a member of the Constitutional Convention as well as a member of the Supreme Court thus rendered his judgment that American citizenship did not derive from the common law.

Clearly the Declaration of Independence was a massive repudiation of the "foedal" doctrine of perpetual allegiance. It would be impossible to maintain that the Founders were adopting the principle of birthright allegiance at the same time that they were dissolving their perpetual allegiance to the King of England. The Declaration of Independence transforms subjects into citizens by making the consent of the governed, not the accident of birth, the ground of citizenship. The principles of the Declaration reject the notion that birth determines subjectship. In its place is the social compact notion of citizenship in which every individual must consent to be governed.

In the *Summary View of the Rights of British America*, Jefferson spoke of the natural right of expatriation as "a right, which nature has given to all men, of departing from the country in which chance, not choice has placed them."[12] Choice, of course, implies reason and the exercise of the right to expatriation depends on reasoned choice, i.e., consent. Chance, however, is the ground of perpetual allegiance. If expatriation is a natural right, then perpetual allegiance—birthright allegiance—is contrary to natural right. A regime based on natural right, one that posits consent

---

11. Chisholm v. Georgia, 2 U.S. (2 Dall.) 419, 456 (1793).
12. Jefferson, "Summary View of the Rights of British America," in *Jefferson: Writings*, Merrill D. Peterson, ed. (New York: Library of America, 1984), 105.

of the governed as its moving principle, cannot ground its citizenship on birthright allegiance or birthright subjectship. This feudal doctrine was repealed by the Declaration of Independence as the "one people" and the "good people" looked elsewhere for the ground of citizenship. The common law did not accord with the basic principles of republican government.

Madison throughout his entire life maintained that "compact, express or implied is the vital principle of free Governments as contradistinguished from Governments not free; and that a revolt against that principle leaves no choice but between anarchy and despotism."[13] As Harry Jaffa has aptly noted, "[t]he idea of compact is at the heart of American constitutionalism. It is at the heart of the philosophical statesmanship that made the Revolution, of which the Constitution is the fruit. In the most fundamental respect, compact is an inference from the proposition 'that all men are created equal'."[14] If compact is the heart of the American Revolution and the Constitution then *eo ipso* it is also the heart of American citizenship.[15] Natural human equality means that no man is by nature the ruler of another and that legitimate rule must therefore be based on the consent of those who are governed. Furthermore, the only legitimate

13. Letter to Daniel Webster, March 15, 1833, in *The Writings of James Madison*, Gaillard Hunt, ed. (New York: G.P. Putnam's Sons, 1900-1910), 9:605. See Letter to N.P. Trist, February, 15, 1830, in ibid., 9:355; "Sovereignty," in ibid., 9:570-571.

14. Harry V. Jaffa, *A New Birth of Freedom: Abraham Lincoln and the Coming of the Civil War* (Lanham: Rowman & Littlefield 2000), 37.

15. See James H. Kettner, *The Development of American Citizenship, 1608-1870* (Chapel Hill: University of North Carolina Press, 1978), 350. For the Revolutionary generation the "principles of liberty" that defined "membership in free community...led inevitably to the conclusion that all legitimate power over men depended upon their own consent to be governed. All citizenship—and not just that which was created by naturalization or revolutionary election—seemed definable in terms of a legal contract between the individual and the community at large."

basis for consent is the better protection of those natural rights which governments do not create but are instituted to protect.

The doctrine of social compact which is intrinsic to the argument of the Declaration was more fully explicated by John Adams in the Massachusetts Bill of Rights (1780):

> The end of the institution, maintenance and administration of government, is to secure the existence of the body politic, to protect it, and to furnish the individuals who compose it with the power of enjoying in safety and tranquility their natural rights...and whenever these great objects are not obtained, the people have a right to alter the government...The body politic is formed by a voluntary association of individuals; it is a social compact by which *the whole people covenants with each citizen and each citizen with the whole people* that all shall be governed by certain laws for the *common good* (emphasis added).

Thus the establishment of civil society requires reciprocal consent. Furthermore, compact must be unanimous; no person can be ruled without his consent. Unanimous consent specifies the ends of government, but majority rule determines the means by which the ends are secured. But, as always, the means must be proportioned to the ends; the majority cannot sacrifice the "safety and tranquility" of the minority or of any individual. As Madison wrote in 1835, majority rule acts only as a "plenary substitute" for the "will of the whole society." Consequently the majority may do anything that could be "rightfully done by unanimous concurrence of the members; the reserved rights of individuals (of conscience for example) in becoming parties to the original compact being beyond the legitimate reach of sovereignty, wherever vested or however viewed."[16]

---

16. *The Writings of James Madison*, 9:570–571.

Majority rule can do only what unanimous consent can *rightly* or justly do. Even unanimous consent cannot rightfully do what is intrinsically unjust. The ends specified in the original compact are thus inviolable.

NATURALIZATION AND SOCIAL COMPACT

Once civil society is established by the voluntary and unanimous consent of its members, it necessarily proceeds by majority rule. New members can be added only with the consent of those who already constitute civil society. Those who were not parties to the original contract remain in the state of nature with respect to the new body politic. As Madison wrote, "in the case of naturalization a new member is added to the social compact, not only without a unanimous consent of the members, but by a majority of the governing body, deriving its powers from a majority of the individual parties to the social compact."[17] No individual can be ruled without his consent nor can any individual join an already established community without the consent of the community. Naturalization is the result of contract—an offer on one side and an acceptance on the other. No community, of course, is obliged to accept new members; the determination to add new members is a matter of prudence and will be dictated by the safety and happiness of the body politic.

Congress has the exclusive power under Article I of the Constitution "To establish an uniform Rule of Naturalization" and a necessary inference from this power is that Congress also has exclusive power to regulate immigration as well as define the qualifications for citizenship. As a practical matter, however, until the adoption of the Fourteenth Amendment state citizenship determined federal citizen-

---

17. Ibid.

ship—those who were citizens of states were automatically deemed citizens of the United States. The states devised various rules and regulations governing naturalization to state citizenship, including oaths of allegiance, tests of moral character and residency requirements. As mentioned earlier, the privileges and immunities clause of Article IV clearly implied a federal citizenship that was independent of state citizenship and presidents must be natural born "citizens of the United States." The privileges and immunities adhered to federal citizenship since the guarantee of protection "in the several States" could not be an incident of state citizenship. For a variety of reasons—most of them having to do with the anomaly of slavery continuing to exist within a regime dedicated to the proposition that "all men are created equal"—the citizenship issue was not definitively addressed until the Fourteenth Amendment. In 1783 Jefferson had written that the slaves were "one half the citizens" of America.[18] Jefferson knew of course that no slave was a citizen of any state; but the logic of the founding—the logic of the principles of the Declaration—looked forward to the inevitable abolition of slavery and the eventual citizenship of those who had been ruled unjustly without their consent.

THE FOURTEENTH AMENDMENT AND CITIZENSHIP

One perceptive commentator has argued that in the debate over the Fourteenth Amendment "the Republican Party was forced to investigate the meaning of citizenship in the nation and the rights which appertained to that status...They defined United States citizenship as incorporating all the civil rights necessary to secure the natural rights of man. They so defined United States citizenship because it was the only

---

18. *Notes on the State of Virginia*, in *Writings*, Query XVIII, 288.

effective way they could apply the principle of the Declaration of Independence."[19] The observation is confirmed by many who debated the issue in the thirty–ninth Congress. One of the most powerful statements to this effect was made by Representative Thaddeus Stevens, a prominent member of the Joint Committee on Reconstruction, on May 8, 1866:

> Consider the magnitude of the task which was imposed upon the committee. They were expected to suggest a plan for rebuilding a shattered nation...It cannot be denied that this terrible struggle sprang from the vicious principles incorporated into the institutions of our country. Our fathers had been compelled to postpone the principles of their great Declaration, and wait for their full establishment till a more propitious time. That time ought to be present now.[20]

Thus, for Stevens, the Fourteenth Amendment was, in some very important sense, a completion of the founding. The founding was incomplete because of the compromises with slavery. Insofar as the Constitution of 1789 tolerated the continued existence of slavery, it remained an incomplete expression of the principles of the Declaration of Independence. The protections for slavery were necessary to purchase the support of the slave–holding states for a strong national government. And as the most perceptive Federalists understood, without a strong national government the prospects of ever being able to end slavery were remote. Madison defended the compromises in the Virginia Ratifying Convention. "Great as the evil is," Madison said, "a dismemberment of the union would be worse." Without protections for slavery "the southern states would not have

---

19. Robert J. Kaczorowski, *The Nationalization of Civil Rights* (New York: Garland Publishing, 1987), 34, 103.
20. *Congressional Globe*, 39th Congress., 1st Sess. 2459 (1866).

entered into the union of America...[a]nd if they were excluded from the union, the consequences might be dreadful to them and to us."[21] These compromises were justified, of course, only to the extent that they were in fact necessary and only to the extent that they provided a foundation for eventual emancipation. The Constitution's grounding in the principles of the Declaration made the eventual abolition of slavery a moral imperative.

On February 15, 1866 Representative William Newell commented on the relation of the Declaration and the Constitution, noting that "[t]he framers of the Constitution did what they considered best under the circumstances. They made freedom the rule and slavery the exception in the organization of the Government. They declared in favor of the former in language the most emphatic and sublime in history, while they placed the latter, as they fondly hoped, in a position favorable for ultimate extinction."[22] Newell here was echoing the words of Abraham Lincoln, whose omnipresent spirit animated the deliberations of the thirty–ninth Congress. Lincoln maintained that the Constitution, understood properly in the light of the principles of the Declaration of Independence, had put slavery "in course of ultimate extinction."[23] The task of the thirty–ninth Congress was not, as some contemporary commentators allege, to frame a new constitution or to perpetrate a constitutional revolution, but to complete the original Constitution by fulfilling the principles of the Declaration.[24] The framers of the Thirteenth

---

21. *The Records of the Federal Convention,* Max Farrand, ed., 3:324–325.
22. *Congressional Globe,* 39th Cong., 1st Sess. 866.
23. Speech at Chicago, July 10, 1858, in *The Collected Works of Abraham Lincoln,* Ray Basler, ed. (New Brunswick: Rutgers University Press, 1953), 2:492; see House Divided Speech, June 16, 1858, in ibid., 2:461.
24. The late Justice Thurgood Marshall said that he did not consider "the wisdom, foresight, and sense of justice exhibited by the Framers particularly profound. To the contrary, the government they devised was

and Fourteenth Amendments looked upon the Civil War as in some sense the second battle of the Revolutionary War. That is to say, they considered the Revolutionary War and the Civil War as two battles in the same war, both battles fought to vindicate the principle that the "just powers of government" are based on the "consent of the governed." The Revolutionary War vindicated that principle for most, but the continued existence of slavery and its recognition in the Constitution rendered the founding incomplete. The Civil War was fought to extend the principle of consent to all the governed and with the adoption of the Reconstruction Amendments, the Constitution for the first time came into formal harmony with the principles of the Declaration of Independence. The idea that the thirty–ninth Congress was engaged in completing the founding was expressed so frequently during debates that one can hardly doubt that it was the ruling paradigm.[25]

Almost everyone seems to agree that the citizenship clause of the Fourteenth Amendment was principally designed to overturn the *Dred Scot* decision (1857). *Dred Scot* had held that no black of African descent, free or slave,

---

defective from the start, requiring several amendments, a civil war, and momentous social transformation to attain the system of constitutional government and its respect for the individual freedoms and human rights, we hold as fundamental today....While the Union survived the civil war, the Constitution did not. In its place arose a new, more promising basis for justice and equality, the 14th Amendment." Speech to the San Francisco Patent and Trademark Law Association, Maui, Hawaii, May 6, 1987, published as "Reflections on the Bicentennial of the United States Constitution," in *Harvard Law Review* 101:1 (1987).

25. In addition to the speeches cited in the text, see *inter alia, Congressional Globe*, 39th Cong., 1st Sess. 571 (Rep. Morrill); 573 (Sen. Trumbull); 574 (Rep. Johnson); 673–674; 680; 682; 684–685 (Sen. Sumner); 726–728 (Rep. Walker); 739 (Sen. Lane); 1012 (Rep. Plants); 1077–1078 (Sen. Nye); 1089 (Rep. Bingham); 1262 (Rep. Broomall); 2510 (Rep. Miller); 2802 (Sen. Stewart); 2961 (Sen. Poland); 3032 (Sen. Johnson); 3037 (Sen. Yates).

could ever be a citizen of the United States. Blacks, Chief Justice Taney had proclaimed, were not included in the Declaration's self-evident truth that "all men are created equal" and as a consequence could not be considered a part of "We the people" who framed and ratified the Constitution. Lincoln, of course, had tirelessly exposed the factual errors upon which Taney's decision rested; principal among them was the fact that in some states free blacks voted in the election to ratify the Constitution and were thus a part of "We the people." Many believed that the Thirteenth Amendment and the Civil Rights Act of 1866 were sufficient to establish the citizenship of the newly freed slaves. But cautious lawmakers wanted an amendment that would unmistakably and unambiguously secure citizenship and put the citizenship status of the newly minted citizens beyond the reach of simple legislative majorities.

Despite its vital importance to the overall scheme of the Fourteenth Amendment, the citizenship clause was a last minute addition to the amendment.

> All persons born or naturalized in the United States, and subject to the jurisdiction thereof, are citizens of the United States and of the State wherein they reside.

Even though there was federal case law upholding the exclusive power of the federal government to define citizenship, prior to the Fourteenth Amendment it had been almost universal practice that federal citizenship was an incident of state citizenship; every citizen of a state was automatically considered to be a citizen of the United States. The Fourteenth Amendment clearly reversed this relationship. Making United States citizenship primary and state citizenship derivative rendered it impossible for the states to prevent newly freed slaves from becoming United States citizens, thus defeating all attempts by the federal government to secure their civil rights.

The citizenship clause contains two requirements: born or naturalized in the United States and subject to the jurisdiction of the United States. Birth within the territorial limits of the United States does not mean that the person is automatically "subject to the jurisdiction" of the United States. Senator Jacob Howard of Ohio, the author of the citizenship clause, noted in debate that "the word 'jurisdiction,' as here employed, ought to be construed so as to imply a full and complete jurisdiction on the part of the United States, coextensive in all respects with the constitutional power of the United States."[26]

Howard was forced to defend the new language against the charge that it would make Indians citizens of the United States. He assured several tenacious and skeptical critics that "Indians born within the limits of the United States, and who maintain their tribal relations, are not in the sense of this amendment, born subject to the jurisdiction of the United States."[27] Senator Lyman Trumbull, chairman of the powerful Senate Judiciary Committee, rose to support his colleague, contending that "subject to the jurisdiction thereof" simply meant "[n]ot owing allegiance to anybody else... subject to the complete jurisdiction of the United States." Indians, he concluded, were not "subject to the jurisdiction" of the United States because they owed allegiance— even if only partial allegiance—to their tribes. Thus two requirements were set for United States citizenship: born or naturalized in the United States *and* subject to its jurisdiction. Birth within the territorial limits of the United States, as the case of the Indians seemed to indicate, did not make one automatically "subject to the jurisdiction" of the United States.

It has often been noted, however, that the language of

---

26. *Congressional Globe,* 39th Cong., 1st Sess. 2895 (Sen. Howard).
27. Ibid., 2890.

the Fourteenth Amendment is "subject to the jurisdiction," not "owing allegiance." "Jurisdiction," we are assured, is a legal term of art, and its meaning can easily be gleaned from a cursory glance at *Black's Law Dictionary*: jurisdiction is "the authority by which courts and judicial officers take cognizance of and decide cases." By this definition, all persons born or naturalized in the United States and subject to its courts and its laws are citizens. Thus it would seem that all persons born in the United States are automatically subject to its jurisdiction regardless of their allegiance, presuming, of course, that the allegiance of children would follow that of their parents. Allegiance, we are assured, contrary to the understanding of Senators Howard and Trumbull, has no relevance to the Fourteenth Amendment's definition of citizenship.

If these two architects of the Fourteenth Amendment meant "allegiance," why didn't they put "subject to the allegiance of the United States" into the amendment instead of "subject to the jurisdiction?" Howard, the author of the citizenship clause, doesn't address this issue in the Fourteenth Amendment debates, but it is not too difficult to guess why he chose the language. "Allegiance," as we have seen, is the common law term; "perpetual allegiance" is the obligation of birthright subjectship. There is credible evidence from the debates over the Civil Rights Act of 1866, however, that its authors specifically intended to avoid common law language when dealing with United States citizenship. Senator Trumbull remarked that his goal in the legislation was

> to make citizens of everybody born in the United States who owe allegiance to the United States. We cannot make a citizen of the child of a foreign minister who is temporarily residing here. There is a difficulty in framing the amendment so as to make citizens of all the people born in the United States and who owe allegiance to it. I thought that might be the best form in which to put the

amendment at one time, "That all persons born in the United States and owing allegiance thereto are hereby declared to be citizens;" but upon investigation it was found that a sort of allegiance was due to the country from persons temporarily resident in it whom we would have no right to make citizens, and that that would not answer.[28]

Trumbull here alludes to the fact that under the common law temporary allegiance is "such as is due from an alien, or stranger born, for so long time as he continues within the king's dominion and protection: and it ceases, the instant such stranger transfers himself from this kingdom to another."[29] Trumbull seems to exclude from the citizenship clause aliens owing only temporary allegiance to the United States and, presumably, in terms of the language of the Fourteenth Amendment, they would not be "subject to the jurisdiction" of the United States, even though subject to its laws and courts. The authors of the Fourteenth Amendment's citizenship clause, I would surmise, simply did not want to include any notion that American citizenship was grounded in the common law, a ground that they knew was utterly inconsistent with the principles of republican government. But Howard was tolerably clear: "subject to the jurisdiction" means complete allegiance to the United States, not by the accident of birth but by consent. "Jurisdiction" was thus a proper republican substitute for "allegiance."

One commentator has accurately, if circumspectly, concluded that the Fourteenth Amendment debates

> establish that the framers of the Citizenship Clause had no intention of establishing a universal rule of birthright citizenship. To be sure, they intended to do more than simply extend citizenship to native-born blacks by overruling the reasoning and result in *Dred Scott*. But they

---

28. Ibid., 572 (Sen. Trumbull).
29. Blackstone, I:358.

also intended, through the clause's jurisdiction requirement, to limit the scope of birthright citizenship. The
essential limiting principle, discernible from the debates
(especially those concerned with the citizenship status of
Native Americans) was consensualist in nature. Citizenship as qualified by this principle, was not satisfied by
mere birth on the soil or by naked governmental power
or legal jurisdiction over the individual. Citizenship required in addition the existence of conditions indicating
mutual consent to political membership.[30]

A severe critic of this view writes that the debates indicate
that the framers of the Fourteenth Amendment intended to
adhere to the common law basis for citizenship. "The debates make it very clear," this critic writes, "that the framers of the Fourteenth Amendment did not view themselves
as adopting revolutionary new principles of citizenship by
consent."[31] It is true that the architects of the Fourteenth
Amendment did not intend to adopt "revolutionary new
principles of citizenship." Rather they were adhering to
the principles of the American founding which, as we have
seen, placed citizenship squarely on the principle of consent. Consent is not a "modern" innovation as our critic
would have us believe; it is rather, as Lincoln said, "our
ancient faith." The Fourteenth Amendment was a restora-
tion of that faith, a completion of the founding by recourse
to first principles.

It is a fundamental principle of constitutional interpretation that no part of the Constitution can be rendered
superfluous or without force by interpretation. This rule
is a necessary ingredient of a written constitution. The

---

30. Peter H. Schuck, *Citizens, Strangers, and In–Betweens: Essays on Immigration and Citizenship* (Boulder: Westview Press, 1998), 213.
31. Gerald L. Neuman, *Strangers to the Constitution: Immigrants, Borders, and Fundamental Law* (Princeton: Princeton University Press,
1996), 175.

American Constitution is a solemn compact between "We the people" in their collective capacity and government. It cannot be changed at will, either by the people or by the government. Article 5 contains procedures for changing the Constitution and no act of mere interpretation can either subtract or add to the Constitution. Rendering some part of the Constitution without force or effect is tantamount to amendment by interpretation.[32] But this is precisely the result of the interpretation which argues that all who are born within the geographical limits of the United States are automatically subject to the jurisdiction of the United States. This interpretation renders the jurisdiction clause superfluous—without force or effect. Had this been the framers'

---

32. Robert Bork writes that the "theory" that "every part of the Constitution must be used" is a fiction invented by judicial activists. Some parts of the Constitution deserve to be ignored, Bork argues, because their "meaning cannot be ascertained." They might as well be "written in Sanskrit or [be] obliterated past deciphering by an ink blot." One such part of the Constitution, he argues, is the "privileges and immunities" clause of the Fourteenth Amendment and presumably the "privileges and immunities" clause of Article 4. These clauses are a "mystery" and should therefore be ignored because the intentions of the framers cannot be determined. Judicial activists take advantage of these "mystery" clauses, according to Bork, because they can exploit their vagueness, using them as a vehicle to write their own ideological predilections into the Constitution. Bork, of course, is famous for justly criticizing judicial decisions that go beyond the constitutional text, structure and history. But what is the difference between the judicial activists who add new provisions that they prefer and the adherents of "original intent jurisprudence" who ignore provisions that they disfavor? It should be obvious that every part of the Constitution must have force and effect as written and that every provision of the Constitution must be interpreted to be compatible with every other part. Judicial activists, however, agree with original intent jurisprudes such as Bork: the Constitution is merely a procedural document devoid of ends or purposes. With this basic agreement both sides can innovate upon the Constitution at will. Some innovations will be unwarranted additions to the Constitution and others will be unwarranted subtractions. Robert H. Bork, *The Tempting of America: The Political Seduction of the Law* (New York: Free Press, 1990), 166.

intent, they would have omitted the jurisdiction clause as simply redundant. Its inclusion obviously means that there are two requirements for citizenship, born or naturalized *and* subject to the jurisdiction and that the mere accident of birth is not sufficient to establish jurisdiction.

As Senator Howard concluded, "jurisdiction" understood in the sense of complete allegiance to the United States "will not, of course, include persons born in the United States who are foreigners, aliens, who belong to the families of ambassadors or foreign ministers."[33] Most remarkable, however, was Senator Howard's contention that "every person born within the limits of the United States, and subject to their jurisdiction, is by virtue of natural law and national law a citizen of the United States."[34] In the context, "national law" refers to "positive law," the law of the Constitution or statutory law. And almost everyone certainly would have understood the phrase "natural law" to refer to the social compact basis of citizenship, the basis for citizenship adumbrated, as we have seen, in the Declaration of Independence and other public documents of the founding era. It is difficult therefore not to conclude that consent was intended by the

---

33. *Congressional Globe*, 39th Cong., 1st Sess. 2890 (Sen. Howard). Some commentators have argued that Howard's statement is ambiguous. Without the comma after "aliens" the phrase could be read as meaning that "foreigners" were exclusively "aliens who belong to the families of ambassadors or foreign ministers." Thus without the comma the phrase would read: "who are foreigners, [that is, those who are] aliens who belong to the families of ambassadors or foreign ministers." The *Congressional Globe* was a transcript of speeches taken by short-hand reporters and the insertion of a comma after "aliens" may have been a mistake. As it stands, however, the meaning is tolerably clear: the children of foreigners, aliens, ambassadors and foreign ministers born in the United States are not "subject to the jurisdiction" of the United States. Senator Howard's statement here is in full agreement with Senator Trumbull's understanding of the citizenship clause of the Civil Rights Act of 1866 quoted above.
34. Ibid. See 2765 (Sen. Howard).

framers of the Fourteenth Amendment to be the foundation of citizenship. The concept of birthright allegiance or "citizenship" was rejected by the Declaration of Independence no less than by the framers of the Fourteenth Amendment.

This conclusion is confirmed by the debate that surrounded the passage of the Expatriation Act of 1868. The act simply provided, in relevant part, that "the right of expatriation is a natural and inherent right of all people, indispensable to the enjoyment of the rights of life, liberty, and the pursuit of happiness." Senator Howard, whose opinion should carry great weight in this debate, stated that the principles of the Declaration of Independence—alluded to in the very language of the act—meant that "the right of expatriation...is inherent and natural in man as man."[35] The notion of birthright citizenship was frequently described as an "indefensible feudal doctrine of indefeasible allegiance." One member of the House of Representatives expressed the general sense of the Congress when he concluded that "[i]t is high time that feudalism were driven from our shores and eliminated from our law, and now is the time to declare it."[36]

Representative Frederick Woodbridge of Vermont, one of the principal proponents of the legislation, argued that the doctrine of perpetual allegiance "is based upon the feudal systems under which there were no free citizens...and the individual man [had] no personal rights; and it was from this source and system that Blackstone derived his idea of indefeasible and perpetual allegiance to the English Crown." But "the old feudal doctrine stated by Blackstone and adopted as part of the common law of England, that

---

35. *Congressional Globe*, 40th Cong., 2nd Sess., Appendix, 561.
36. Ibid., 868 (Rep. Woodward); Representative Bailey of New York described birthright citizenship as "the slavish feudal doctrine of perpetual allegiance," at 967. Similar arguments were frequently voiced throughout the debate.

once a citizen by the accident of birth expatriation under any circumstances less than the consent of the sovereign is an impossibility. The doctrine...is not only at war with the theory of our institutions, but is equally at war with every principle of justice and of sound public law."[37] With the passage of the Expatriation Act of 1868, it seemed that birthright citizenship or allegiance had finally been banished from the American regime. Representative Woodbridge's unequivocal repudiation of Blackstone makes it almost impossible to maintain that, after the passage of the Expatriation Act, the common law was the basis of American citizenship. Expatriation, of course, is inconsistent with the idea of "perpetual ligeance." But if it is true, as Jefferson remarked, that expatriation is a natural right derived from the principles of natural law, then perpetual allegiance and birthright citizenship are alien to the principles of the Declaration. It is difficult to believe that the framers of the Fourteenth Amendment intended to adopt the common law rule of citizenship in the light of their many protestations that citizenship derived from consent.

In 1870, the Senate Judiciary Committee issued a report confirming that the primary intention of the Fourteenth Amendment was to secure the citizenship of the newly freed slaves and was not intended to confer citizenship on American Indians.[38] Shortly thereafter the Congress began passing legislation offering citizenship to individual members of Indian tribes. Members of specified tribes, first the Winnebagos, then the Miami tribe of Kansas, could accept the offer of citizenship by consenting to the terms of the offer. Here Congress used its powers under section 5 of the Fourteenth Amendment to render the members of these tribes "subject to the jurisdiction" of the United States. Finally, the Indian

---

37. Ibid., 1130–1131.
38. *Senate Report No. 268*, 41st Cong., 3rd Sess. (1870).

Citizenship Act of 1924 extended the offer to all Native Persons in the United States. Since the citizenship clause of the Fourteenth Amendment does not impose any restrictions on the states, the requirement developed in Supreme Court doctrine in later years that Congress under section 5 can act only in a remedial context, does not apply. Congress, it seems, has plenary power to specify the reach of the jurisdiction clause and was clearly exercising this power in extending jurisdiction to Native Persons, those born within the geographical boundaries of the United States but not "subject to the jurisdiction" of the United States.

NATIVE PERSONS AND THE REQUIREMENT OF RECIPROCAL CONSENT: ELK V. WILKINS

The Supreme Court first took up the issue in *Elk v. Wilkins* (1884). In this case, Elk had renounced his tribal allegiance and had lived apart from his tribe for a year. The record did not indicate which tribe Elk had been born into but according to the Court the record "clearly implies" that the tribe "still exists and is recognized as a Tribe by the Government of the United States."[39] Elk alleged that he had "completely surrendered himself to the jurisdiction of the United States" and therefore was a citizen of the United States.[40] As the Court noted, however, Elk made no claim that the United States had accepted or recognized his surrender of tribal allegiance, nor did he allege "that he has ever been naturalized or taxed or in any way recognized or treated as a citizen, by the State [of Nebraska] or by the United States." The Court was adamant that the ascription of citizenship could not be a unilateral or self-selected act: "The alien and

---

39. Elk v. Wilkins, 112 U.S. 94, 99 (1884).
40. Ibid.

dependent condition of the members of the Indian Tribes," the Court concluded, "could not be put off at their own will, without the action or assent of the United States" signified either by treaty or legislation. Neither "the Indian Tribes" nor "individual members of those Tribes," no more than "other foreigners" can "become citizens of their own will." Native persons and immigrants "from any foreign State" must first proffer "a formal renunciation" of all former allegiance and then await "an acceptance by the United States of that renunciation through such form of naturalization as may be required by law."[41]

Thus, in the Court's interpretation, consent must be reciprocal. No one can be made a citizen against his will nor can anyone become a citizen without the consent of those who already constitute the body politic. This illustrates the constitutional "principle" which is inherent in the idea of sovereignty "that no one can become a citizen of a Nation without its consent."[42] Justice Gray's majority opinion thus almost reads as a commentary on the Massachusetts Bill of Rights quoted above. He rightly understood that the framers of the Constitution, no less than the framers of the Fourteenth Amendment, grounded citizenship in social compact. As we have seen, Congress had extended legislative offers of citizenship to individual members of Indian tribes, thus bringing those individuals within the jurisdiction of the United States and making them eligible for naturalization. But as the Court noted these "several Acts for naturalizing Indians of certain Tribes" would be entirely "superfluous if they were or might become, without any action of the government, citizens of the United States."[43] Thus the existence of these legislative proffers indicates that members

---

41. Ibid. at 101.
42. Ibid. at 103.
43. Ibid. at 104.

of Indian tribes cannot become "subject to the jurisdiction" of the United States of their own volition.

It might also be argued that amnesty provisions, such as those contained in the Immigration Reform and Control Act of 1986, are also exercises of congressional power under section 5 of the Fourteenth Amendment, extending the jurisdiction of the United States to illegal aliens residing in the United States. Surely those who come to the United States illegally—while they may be under the jurisdiction of the courts and subject to the laws of the United States— cannot confer jurisdiction upon themselves *sua sponte* any more than Elk. It would be difficult—if not utterly impossible—to argue that breaking the laws of the United States is sufficient to confer jurisdiction in the sense of not owing allegiance to any other country, since it is clear that crossing the border illegally demonstrates no allegiance whatsoever to the laws of the United States. Amnesty is required to confer jurisdiction in the case of those in the country illegally, and no one doubts Congress' authority to do so. Since there were no illegal immigrants in the country in 1866 it is not surprising that the question of illegal immigration never arose during the debates over the Fourteenth Amendment. But it is not particularly difficult to determine from the principles incorporated into the citizenship clause what the conclusion of the debate would have been: reciprocal consent is the sine qua non of American citizenship. In the case of children born to illegal immigrants, their allegiance would follow that of their parents, as in the case of Native Persons born into a tribe. It would be difficult to argue that an illegal act is sufficient to confer the boon of citizenship on the children of such law–breakers. Those who support automatic citizenship for the children of illegal aliens demand for them what everyone agrees was not extended to Native Persons by the Fourteenth Amendment.

Justice Harlan penned an interesting dissent in *Elk*. He apparently agreed with the principles articulated by the majority decision that the basis of citizenship was reciprocal consent, but he disagreed about the particular application of the facts in *Elk*. Harlan inferred from the record that Elk was a *bona fide* resident of the state of Nebraska and as such would have been subject to taxes. "[W]e submit," Harlan wrote, "that the petition does sufficiently show that the plaintiff is taxed, that is, belongs to the class which, by the laws of Nebraska, is subject to taxation." In fact, according to Harlan, Elk "has become so far incorporated with the mass of the people of Nebraska that, being, as the petition avers, a citizen and resident thereof, he constitutes a part of her militia." As a *bona fide* resident he is also "counted in every apportionment of representation in the Legislature" which the Nebraska Constitution stipulates excludes only "Indians not taxed." In fact, Harlan points out, only "Indians not taxed" were excluded from the enumeration determining the apportionment of federal Representatives. Since "at the adoption of the Constitution there were, in many of the States, Indians, not members of any Tribe" they were "Indians taxed" and included in the enumeration. The same rule, Harlan contends "is preserved in the 14th Amendment; for now, as at the adoption of the Constitution, Indians in the several States, who are taxed by their laws, are counted in establishing the basis of representation in Congress."[44]

Harlan pointed out that the Civil Rights Act of 1866 extended citizenship to all except "Indians not taxed." Since there were many Indians who had severed relations with their tribes and were subject to taxation, the ineluctable inference is that taxed Indians were made citizens by the operation of that legislation. Harlan concluded that the

----

44. Ibid. at 111–112.

Fourteenth Amendment, although it did not include the phraseology of the Civil Rights Act, nevertheless rested on the same distinction between Indians taxed and not taxed.

> A careful examination of all that was said by Senators and Representatives, pending the consideration by Congress of the 14th Amendment, justifies us in saying that everyone who participated in the debates, whether for or against the Amendment, believed that in the form in which it was approved by Congress it granted and was intended to grant national citizenship to every person of the Indian race in this country who was unconnected with any Tribe and who resided, in good faith, outside of Indian reservations and within one of the States or Territories of the Union.[45]

Harlan seems to argue that in Elk's case the fact that he was a taxpayer and subject to other obligations indicated a kind of tacit consent to his allegiance on the part of Nebraska and the United States and that this tacit consent effectively made Elk "subject to the jurisdiction" of the United States. The majority, on the other hand, seemed to argue that as long as the tribe an Indian was born into retained its political existence there could be no self–selected renunciation of tribal allegiance. Only if the tribe was disbanded and its members scattered among the general population could there be the tacit recognition of allegiance. The majority did not believe that was in fact the case with Elk, although the record did not settle the issue definitively.

Harlan considered the Senate report of 1870 as a definitive statement of the meaning of the jurisdiction clause. The report concluded that generally the Fourteenth Amendment excluded Indians who maintained allegiance to their tribes but that "when the members of any Indian Tribe are scattered, they are merged in the mass of our people and become

---

45. Ibid. at 118.

equally subject to the jurisdiction of the United States."[46]
This, in Harlan's view, was precisely Elk's situation.

UNITED STATES v. WONG KIM ARK

In the case of *U.S. v. Wong Kim Ark* (1898), however, the
Court retreated from the reasoning of *Elk*. In this case a ma-
jority of the Court, over a powerful dissent from the Chief
Justice, joined by Justice Harlan, held that the Fourteenth
Amendment explicitly adopted the common law basis for
citizenship.

Wong Kim Ark was born to parents who were legally
permanent residents of the United States but remained subjects of China and retained their allegiance to the Emperor.
As the result of a treaty between the United States and China they were rendered ineligible for American citizenship.
The question was whether Wong Kim Ark was an American
citizen solely by virtue of his birth within the territorial
limits of the United States.

Justice Gray, writing for the majority, noted that the first
section of the Fourteenth Amendment, no less than other provisions of the Constitution, "must be interpreted in
the light of the common law, the principles and history of
which were familiarly known to the framers of the Constitution....The language of the Constitution...could not be
understood without reference to the common law."[47] Thus,
Gray concludes,

> [t]he real object of the 14th Amendment of the Constitu-
> tion, in qualifying the words, "all persons born in the
> United States," by the addition, "and subject to the juris-
> diction thereof," would appear to have been to exclude, by
> the fewest and fittest words (besides children of members

---

46. Ibid. at 119.
47. United States v. Wong Kim Ark, 169 U.S. 649, 654 (1898).

of the Indian tribes, standing in a peculiar relation to the
national government, unknown to the common law) the
two classes of cases—children born of alien enemies in
hostile occupation, and children of diplomatic representatives of a foreign state—both of which, as has already
been shown by the law of England, and by our own law,
from the time of the first settlement of the English colonies in America, had been recognized exceptions to the
fundamental rule of citizenship by birth within the country [citing *inter alia Calvin's Case*].[48]

Gray does not provide any argument justifying his position
that the common law controls the interpretation of the Constitution. Everyone will concede that "the principles and
history" of the common law "were familiarly known to the
framers of the Constitution," but this hardly constitutes
proof that they intended the Constitution to be an expression of common law principles. I believe that Madison and
most other framers would have been surprised by this casual assumption. Madison described arguments asserting
that the common law was a part of American law and the
Constitution of the United States as "pretensions" which
were "absolutely destitute of foundation." Indeed, Madison argues, "no support nor colour can be drawn from [our
revolution] for the doctrine that the common law is binding
on these states as one society. The doctrine on the contrary,
is evidently repugnant to the fundamental principle of the
revolution."[49] Surely Madison considered the common law
doctrine of "birthright ligeance" as utterly "repugnant" to
the natural right principles of the American Revolution.

James Wilson, another framer, argued in a similar vein.
Blackstone and the Constitution, he maintained, "set out
from different points of departure [in] regard to the very

---

48. Ibid. at 682.
49. *The Papers of James Madison*, David B. Matern, et al., eds. (Charlot-
tesville: University Press of Virginia, 1991) 17:328.

first principles of government." Blackstone cannot be considered "a friend of republicanism" for the simple reason that he did not support the right of revolution, the "principle of the Constitution of the United States, and of every State of the Union." In other words, Blackstone did not recognize the right of revolution, as did Wilson and the other framers, as the right that guaranteed all other rights. As Blackstone casually mentioned, when "Mr. Locke" speaks of "at once an entire dissolution of the bands of government" he "perhaps carries his theory too far."[50] For the framers—as for Locke—consent of the governed was the active principle of republican government, continuously operative through democratic elections, but ultimately resting on the principle that the people always reserve the natural right of revolution.

Blackstone had, of course, written of the "original compact of society," but in his view the "original compact" was incompatible with the right to revolution.[51] Blackstone doubted that "the original contract of society...has ever been formally expressed at the first institution of a state," "yet in nature and reason [it] must always be understood and implied in the very act of associating together." The "original contract" embodies the principle that "the whole should protect all its parts, and that every part should pay obedience to the will of the whole; or in other words, that the community should guard the rights of each individual member, and that (in return for this protection) each individual should submit to the laws of the community; without which submission of all it was impossible that protection could be certainly extended to any."[52] Once society

---

50. Blackstone, I.52.
51. See Michael P. Zuckert, *Launching Liberalism: On Lockean Political Philosophy* (Lawrence: University Press of Kansas, 2002), 257.
52. Blackstone, I.47-48.

is formed, "government results…as necessary to preserve and to keep the society in order." A "state," Blackstone explains, "is a collective body, composed of a multitude of individuals, united for their safety and convenience, and intending to act together as one man" through "one uniform will." But this "political union" can only be produced "by the consent of all persons to submit their own private wills to the will of one man, or of one or more assemblies of men, to whom the supreme authority is entrusted."[53] For the establishment of the supreme authority, consent is necessary, but only for its establishment. Those who are born into this state are not ruled by consent—they owe perpetual birthright allegiance from their birth. Consent is not the active agency for regimes based on the "original contract." And here, it is likely that Blackstone agreed with Coke's formulation of the "original contract" in *Calvin's Case*: natural allegiance is due from subjects born within the protection of the king, "for as the subject oweth to the king his true and faithful ligeance and obedience, so the sovereign is to govern and protect his subjects…so as between the sovereign and subject there is 'duplex et reciprocum ligamen'."[54] The original contract was binding and unrepealable. The "original contract" entailed future generations and was the basis for subjectship. But surely no one could argue that subjectship survived the American Revolution any more than the common law of primogeniture and entail.

It is true that the idea of consent as the new ground and principle of citizenship took time to work its way into the regime as a matter of practice, especially since the question of citizenship was always complicated by issues of federalism and slavery. Justice Gray was able to point to several cases and commentators arguing the common law basis of

---

53. Ibid., I.52.
54. Calvin's Case, at 614.

American citizenship. I believe, however, that all these citations are at best ambiguous and at worst mistaken about the principles of the American Revolution. For example Gray cites Kent's *Commentaries* to this effect:

> And if, at common law, all human beings born within the ligeance of the King, and under the King's obedience, were natural born subjects, and not aliens, I do not perceive why this doctrine does not apply to these United States, in all cases in which there is no express constitutional or statute declaration to the contrary..."Subject" and "citizen" are, in a degree convertible terms as applied to natives; and though the term *citizen* seems to be appropriate to republican freemen, yet we are, equally with the inhabitants of all other countries, *subjects*, for we are equally bound by allegiance and subjection to the government and law of the land.[55]

But of course "subjects" and "citizens" are not convertible terms any more than monarchical government and republican government are convertible because they both are sovereign. This is a doctrine that would please Thomas Hobbes who argued that since all regimes were sovereign the differences between regime forms were insignificant.

The American framers, in contrast, were acutely aware of the importance of regime differences; any form not derived from the consent of the governed was not a legitimate form of government. They were convinced that the only form of government appropriate for Americans was one that was "strictly republican," as Madison wrote in *The Federalist,* because "no other form would be reconcilable with the genius of the people of America; with the fundamental principles of the Revolution; or with that honorable determination which animates every votary of freedom to

---

55. Wong Kim Ark, at 655 (quoting *Kent's Commentaries* 2:258, note).

rest all our political experiments on the capacity of mankind for self–government."[56] In the center of this enumeration is the recognition that only the republican form of government is compatible with the "fundamental principles of the Revolution." If the principles of the Revolution are the point of departure, then *eo ipso* birthright ligeance must be rejected as the basis for American citizenship.

Gray also quoted Justice Story's opinion from *Inglis v. The Trustees of Sailor's Snug Harbor* (1830) as support for the proposition that the Constitution adopted the common law definition of citizenship. After describing in detail the common law basis for discriminating between subjects and aliens, Story declaims with marvelous understatement that "[t]he case of the separation of the United States from Great Britain is, perhaps, not brought within any of the descriptions" contained in the common law. The Declaration of Independence "proclaimed the colonies free and independent States" thus absolving the colonists "from all allegiance to the British crown." The perpetual allegiance of the common law had been overthrown. Yet, Story observed, "it could not escape the notice of the eminent men of that day that most distressing questions must arise; who were to be considered as constituting the American States on the one side, and 'the State of Great Britain' on the other? The common law furnished no perfect guide, or rather, admitted of different interpretations."[57] As Story indicates, the practical

---

56. Alexander Hamilton, James Madison, and John Jay, *The Federalist Papers*, No. 39, Clinton Rossiter, ed. (New York: New American Library, 1961), 240.

57. Inglis v. Trustees of Sailor's Snug Harbor, 28 U.S. (3 Peters) 99, 159 (1830). In the previous year, writing for the Court, Story had opined that "[t]he common law of England is not to be taken in all respects to be that of America. Our ancestors brought with them its general principles, and claimed it as their birthright; but they brought with them and adopted only that portion which was applicable to their situation." Van Ness v. Packard 27 U.S. (2 Peters) 137 (1829). Similar analysis was provided by

implementation of citizenship based on the principle of consent would be difficult. In actual practice the new form of citizenship had to draw on some elements of the common law. Citizenship based on social compact would draw on the principles of *jus soli* as its point of departure, but it would require consent as its active agency, thus rejecting any notion of perpetual allegiance. Allegiance would take on the volitional character of the social compact and the right of expatriation—something impossible on common law grounds—would have to become part of the calculus of American citizenship. The majority opinion in *Wong Kim Ark* acknowledged the right of expatriation, even quoting the Expatriation Act of 1868, which affirmed that expatriation is "a natural and inherent right of all people."[58] Justice Gray did not seem to take cognizance of the fact that this natural right is inherently incompatible with the common law which requires perpetual allegiance.

Kettner has written that transforming the social compact theory of citizenship into practice was complicated by the peculiar circumstances of American politics, principally the

---

Justice M'Lean in Wheaton v. Peters, 33 U.S. (8 Peters) 591, 658 (1834): "It is clear there can be no common law of the United States....There is no principle which pervades the Union and has the authority of law that is not embodied in the Constitution or laws of the Union. The common law could be made a part of our federal system only by legislative adoption." Jefferson captured the spirit in which the founding generation viewed the common law when he remarked in *Notes on the State of Virginia* that "Civil government being the sole object of forming societies, its administration must be conducted by common consent. Every species of government has its specific principles. Ours perhaps are more peculiar than those of any other in the universe. It is a composition of the freest principles of the English constitution, with others derived from natural right and natural reason. To these nothing can be more opposed than the maxims of absolute monarchy." Query VIII, in *Jefferson: Writings*, 211. Presumably "the freest principles of the English constitution" are to be judged from the perspective of natural right.

58. Wong Kim Ark, at 704.

questions of federalism and the presence of slavery. "The first and residual uncertainty," Kettner writes, stemmed from the fact that "[t]he federal system created in 1789 both reflected the continued viability and authority of the individual states and gave legal force and substance to an already pervasive sense of a wider national community... American citizenship implied membership in both state and nation, but the relationship between these two aspects of the status remained the topic of frequent and increasingly heated debate."[59] Although the Constitution gave Congress exclusive power to pass uniform rules on naturalization,[60] as a practical matter the citizens of each state were automatically considered citizens of the United States. In theory, federal citizenship was primary and state citizenship derivate, but in practice it was just the opposite. The extent to which questions of the federal relation were intimately bound up with issues of slavery and the extension of slavery into the territories, the question of the primacy of federal citizenship could not be raised directly any more than the slavery question could. In an amazing understatement, Kettner writes that a "second factor complicating the situation was the presence of the black man in American society."[61] Free blacks who were state citizens, of course, were guaranteed all the privileges and immunities of citizens of the several states by Article IV of the Constitution, although enforcement of those rights in the slave states was politically unthinkable. Thus, Kettner concludes, "[n]ot logic, but force, finally answered these questions. The triumph of the Union in the Civil War and the passage of the postwar amendments brought a fundamental coherence to the law."[62]

---

59. James H. Kettner, *The Development of American Citizenship*, 350.
60. See Chirac v. Chirac, 15 U.S. (2 Wheat.) 259, 269 (1817).
61. Kettner, 350.
62. Ibid., 351.

Chief Justice Fuller, joined by Justice Harlan, wrote a powerful dissent in *Wong Kim Ark* rejecting the majority's holding that the citizenship clause of the Fourteenth Amendment rested on the common law. The rule of birthright subjectship, Fuller rightly noted, "was the outcome of the connection in feudalism between the individual and the soil on which he lived," and "indissoluble" allegiance was due the Crown for protection at birth. But Fuller argues that this feudal notion was rejected by the framers and Founders: "from the Declaration of Independence to this day the United States have rejected the doctrine of indissoluble allegiance."[63] Indeed, the American Revolution itself was a massive rejection of the idea of "indissoluble allegiance." And, of course, the Chief Justice is correct in arguing that the right of expatriation precludes the idea that the common law informed the principles of American citizenship.

Fuller's conclusion is, I believe, irresistible. Under the terms of the Fourteenth Amendment to become a citizen at birth or to be naturalized one must be subject to the complete jurisdiction of the United States. Wong Kim Ark's parents owed allegiance to the Emperor of China and could not by treaty become citizens of the United States. Because of their professed allegiance and incapacity to become citizens they were admittedly not subject to the jurisdiction of the United States, although they were permanent residents. In what sense then can it be maintained that Wong Kim Ark was born into the complete allegiance of the United States? At birth Wong Kim Ark could not owe allegiance to the United States in any real sense and his allegiance would presumably follow that of his parents as it did in the case of Elk, whose parents maintained allegiance to their tribe. The conclusion is inescapable: Wong Kim Ark was born

---

63. Wong Kim Ark, at 706, 711.

outside the jurisdiction of the United States but within its territorial limits.

It is difficult to reconcile Justice Gray's opinion in *Wong Kim Ark* with his analysis in *Elk*. Justice Gray himself gives no indication that he is aware of any tensions between the two decisions. But surely his decision in *Elk* did not rely on the common law since the notion of "domestic dependent nations" was unknown to the common law and was exclusively a creation of American constitutional law. Presumably, children born to Native Persons would be analogous to children born to ambassadors, one of the exceptions to birthright allegiance specified in the common law. But Indian tribes are not sovereign nations, although they do have some of the characteristics of sovereignty. In any case, Gray believed that the question presented in *Wong Kim Ark* could be decided solely by appeal to a common law understanding of the language of the Fourteenth Amendment. In my judgment, however, the two opinions are irreconcilable. The idea that citizenship derives from "reciprocal consent" is, as we have seen, incompatible with the common law basis of subjectship, but is at the heart of the social contract basis of citizenship. In *Elk* Gray was emphatic: no one could become a citizen of the United States without its explicit permission. In *Wong Kim Ark* he presumably concluded that permission was given when Wong Kim Ark's parents were admitted to the country. Implicit in their admittance, apparently, was permission on the part of the United States to consider any children born to them while residents of the United States to be citizens by birth. Yet, Gray admits that Wong Kim Ark "might himself, after coming of age, renounce this citizenship, and become a citizen of the country of his parents, or of any other country."[64]

---

64. Ibid., at 704.

Under the common law, of course, allegiance could not be terminated or transferred except with the permission of the sovereign. Gray might further argue, however, that the Expatriation Act of 1868, which he quotes and acknowledges protects "a natural and inherent right,"[65] confers the general permission of the United States to transfer allegiance at will. But this line of reasoning would be utterly incompatible with the common law.

Since the decision in *Wong Kim Ark* it has been assumed that all persons born within the geographical limits of the United States are automatically citizens of the United States, regardless of whether or not the parents are within the jurisdiction of the United States or whether or not the parents have legal residence in the United States. Although the language of the majority opinion in *Wong Kim Ark* seems capacious enough to include the children of illegal aliens, there has been no decision that I am aware of explicitly holding that the children of illegal aliens are automatically accorded birthright citizenship. Any language in *Wong Kim Ark* that suggests the majority reasoning could be expanded to include the children of illegal immigrants would, of course, be mere dicta since Wong Kim Ark's parents were in the country legally.[66] Even if the logic is that Wong Kim Ark became a citizen by birth with the permission of the United States when it admitted his parents to the country, no such permission has been given to those who enter illegally. If no one can become a citizen without the permission of the United States, then children of illegal aliens must surely be excluded from acquiring birthright citizenship.

---

65. Ibid.
66. The Supreme Court, in dicta, has on occasion casually assumed that a child of illegal aliens "born in the United States" is "a citizen of this country." INS v. Rios–Pineda, 471 U.S. 444, 446 (1985).

POSTMODERN CITIZENSHIP

Advanced liberal opinion maintains that the idea of sovereignty—and hence, the notion of exclusive allegiance—is anachronistic in an increasingly globalized world and should therefore be banished from international norms. Human dignity, we are assured, adheres directly to the individual, and should not require the mediation of the nation–state. Demands made on behalf of the nation–state for exclusive allegiance or for assimilation are contrary to respect for "universal personhood." The nation–state, it is argued, has been rendered irrelevant by globalization and the inevitable world–wide triumph of liberal democracy will eventually render citizenship itself superfluous if not dangerous.

One intellectual has noted that "[c]itizenship, almost universally regarded as the domestic designation of nationality, was (and still is in many respects in most countries) the cornerstone of the nation–state. With the devaluation of citizenship in the United States and in Western Europe, the concept of nationality is being recast from an expression of national self–determination to a legal device for protecting individual human rights. This has dramatic implications for state, society, and the international order."[67] One of the principal causes of the decline in citizenship based on the nation–state, according to this author, is "that the state has lost control of international migration. The transnational ties that have developed, as a consequence, between the aliens and their associations and groups in the host society have had the effect of loosening state–society ties....[T]ransnational ties cut across the vertical ties of the

---

67. David A. Jacobson, *Rights Across Borders: Immigration and the Decline of Citizenship* (Baltimore: Johns Hopkins University Press, 1997), 70.

nation–state." "Most important," this luminary concludes, "the fundamental relationship between state and citizen is broken."[68]

President George W. Bush in some sense agrees with this cosmopolitan view; he has long advocated greater "compassion for our neighbors to the south." After all, the President frequently states, "family values do not stop at the border." Illegal immigrants are merely seeking to support their families and improve their lives. Borders, in the President's view, should not stand in the way of "family values"—those universal "values" that refuse to recognize the importance or relevance of mere political boundaries. By becoming a more "welcoming" society—by ceasing to act as a nation-state—Bush claims, we will become a "more decent" people as well. Somehow exclusivity and the requirement of complete allegiance stand against universal values and universal personhood, not to say human decency.

A sign of the decline of American citizenship and America's decline as a nation–state is its casual acceptance of dual citizenship. Dual citizenship involves multiple allegiances. The framers of the Fourteenth Amendment said citizenship meant exclusive allegiance—"[n]ot owing allegiance to anybody else...subject to the complete jurisdiction of the United States." Indeed, a pledge of exclusive allegiance is still required of the oath of citizenship, although State Department practices allow dual citizenship. Eighty–five percent of all immigrants arriving in America come from countries that allow—indeed encourage—dual citizenship.[69] Dual citizens, of course, give the sending countries a political presence in the United States and many countries use their dual

68. Ibid., 71, 43, 80, 83, 88, 95, 113.
69. Stanley A. Renshon, *The 50% American: Immigration and National Identity in an Age of Terror* (Washington, D.C.: Georgetown University Press, 2005), 184.

citizens to promote their own interests by exerting pressure on American politicians and policymakers. We have the impossible situation where a newly naturalized citizen can swear exclusive allegiance to the United States but retain his allegiance to a vicious despotism or a theocratic tyranny. What is more, dual citizens can serve in the military of the sending nation and can even serve in appointed and elected offices in their original country. Such dual allegiance, of course, is impossible, and the absurdity of this situation is manifest to all except those minions of the administrative state who oversee our naturalization policies.

Cosmopolitans encourage a world system of multiple citizenships where all citizens would also have multiple allegiances. But in a system of multiple allegiances, no one would have any allegiance properly so called. The advocates of universal citizenship believe that the proliferation of multiple citizenships will ultimately lead to the world homogeneous state of free and equal citizens who, as citizens of the world, will possess "universal personhood," rather than the privileges and immunities of a particular regime. But, as Leo Strauss convincingly demonstrated, the universal homogeneous state will not be a universal democracy; rather, it will of necessity be a universal tyranny.[70] This tyranny will have the advantage of having rendered superfluous all questions of citizenship and immigration.

In his 2004 Inaugural speech, President Bush announced that "it is the policy of the United States to seek and support the growth of democratic movements and institutions in every nation and culture, with the ultimate goal of ending tyranny in our world." Support for democratic movements is, of course, a laudable policy when it serves the interests of the United States. But the idea that tyranny can be ended

---

70. Leo Strauss, *On Tyranny* (New York: Free Press, 1991), 193, 208, 211.

in "our world" is simply utopian—and dangerous. If, as Strauss maintained, "tyranny is a danger coeval with political life,"[71] then ending tyranny in the world would require the vision of a radically transformed human nature, where human beings have liberated themselves from all desire for tyranny—indeed from all political life. And regimes inspired by this view of liberated human nature have no reason for moderation—any moderation in the pursuit of perfection must be seen as a vice or a defect. In other words, a particular kind of tyranny—the universal homogeneous state—will be necessary to end tyranny in "our world."

Liberal democracy and the rule of law have historically existed only in nation–states. But we are assured that the universal state devoted to the care and protection of "universal personhood" will liberate the world from the stifling parochialism of the nation–state. The universal homogeneous state, we are told, will preside at the end of history when human nature has emerged from the realm of necessity into the realm of freedom, when human nature has been liberated from all "social constructions." The temptation to intervene in the historical dialectic, to hasten its "inevitable" outcome by the judicious use of force and violence against the most recalcitrant parts of human nature, has proven to be overwhelming. How can the history of the violence–wracked twentieth century be explained except as attempts to secure here and now what the historical dialectic has promised sometime in the remote future? Liberation will often require that human nature be terrorized into compliance. Freedom and dignity have been revealed to be mere delusions, social constructions of various sorts. Terror is required to dispel these mass delusions and only when the instruments of terror can be monopolized by the

71. Ibid., 22, 20; Leo Strauss, *The City and Man* (Chicago: Rand McNally & Co., 1964), 127.

world homogeneous state can the real work of liberation be completed.[72]

The continued vitality of liberal constitutionalism in a system of nation–states is the only guard—and the best guard—against universal tyranny. But the continued vitality of the nation–state depends on the continuing vitality of citizenship which carries with it exclusive allegiance to a "separate and equal" nation. When citizenship is debased and diluted the nation–state is imperiled. A system of nation–states, in which at least some states will be sanctuaries of freedom, would seem to be preferable to universal tyranny. An acute observer writes that "[i]n the modern world, sovereignty has been closely associated with constitutional government, at least in the sense that constitutional government has only been achieved in sovereign states. And it is only in the modern practice of constitutional government that guarantees of personal liberty have been combined with political structures capable of sustaining stable democracy."[73] One otherwise sober commentator supports a limited view of dual citizenship as a necessary response to inevitable globalization. While he believes that "as a practical matter, the nation–state remains the primary vehicle for protecting rights and practicing democracy," he nevertheless asserts that multiple citizenships might be a "prudent," albeit "perilous," method of "extending democratic values and political rule" in the world. "Plural citizenship," our commentator alleges, "supports individuals' commitments to multiple polities and peoples, thus enlarging communal identity in the wake of economic and political globalization.

---

72. See Edward Erler, *The American Polity: Essays on the Theory and Practice of Constitutional Government* (New York: Crane Russak, 1991), ix–xi.
73. Jeremy A. Rabkin, *Law Without Nations? Why Constitutional Government Requires Sovereign States* (Princeton: Princeton University Press, 2005), 16, 239, 254

It facilitates the spread of transnational communities of descent, diasporic communities in their home countries."[74] We are warned, however, that "plural citizenship risks exacerbating the process of alienation and fragmentation already at work in the United States." However it is sold, the promotion of multiple citizenships has as its *terminus ad quo* the universal homogeneous state where there will be subjects but no citizens. Globalization may, in some sense, be a fated fact. Global tyranny, on the other hand, will result from human choice.

---

74. Noah Pickus, *True Faith and Allegiance: Immigration and American Civic Nationalism* (Princeton: Princeton University Press, 2005), 148, 181.

Chapter 3

IMMIGRATION: THE FOUNDERS' VIEW AND TODAY'S CHALLENGE

Thomas G. West*

Does America's national dedication to the proposition that all men are created equal require the borders to be open to all comers? The famous poem inscribed on the Statue of Liberty seems to say so: "Give me your tired, your poor, / Your huddled masses yearning to breathe free."[1] Liberals and libertarians generally favor few or no restrictions on immigration, claiming that the American principles of liberty and equality would otherwise be violated.

Many conservatives agree. The editorial page of the *Wall Street Journal* has lobbied for many years for open borders on the ground that this is what America's principles demand. *Journal* op-ed writer Daniel Henninger insists that Americans who "understand their heritage" oppose sending illegal immigrants back to their homelands. Those who would send them home, writes Henninger, are following

*For their generous support that helped to make possible the research and writing of this paper, the author would like to thank the Claremont Institute, Aequus Institute, and the William M. Bowen Educational Charitable Trust. For help with the editing, I thank Douglas Jeffrey and Denis Ambrose.
1. Emma Lazarus, "The New Colossus," in *Emma Lazarus: Selected Poems*, John Hollander, ed. (New York: Library of America, 2005), 58.

their "darkest impulses." Scholars like Julian Simon provide intellectual support for this position. President George W. Bush has long been a strong advocate of nearly unlimited immigration.[2]

On the other side, traditionalist conservatives reject the idea that American identity is defined by a common creed according to which all persons possess the equal rights to life, liberty, and property, and that government's purpose is

---

2. Daniel Henninger, "A Nation of (Numerous) Laws: Immigration foes just want a little respect," *Wall Street Journal*, March 31, 2006, op-ed page, http://www.opinionjournal.com/columnists/dhenninger/ ?id = 110008165 (accessed April 1, 2006). Robert L. Bartley, "Open Nafta Borders? Why Not? Immigration Is What Made This Country Great," *Wall Street Journal*, July 2, 2001, http://www.opinionjournal.com/columnists/rbartley/?id = 95000738 (accessed August 2, 2005) (in which Bartley repeated his 1984 proposed constitutional amendment, "There shall be open borders"). More recently, "Borderline Republicans: the Internal GOP Battle over Immigration Gets Ugly," unsigned "Review and Outlook" op-ed, *Wall Street Journal*, June 17, 2004, http://www. opinionjournal.com/editorial/feature.html?id = 110005227 (accessed July 8 2005) (hinting that opponents of mass immigration have a hidden "white-supremacist" agenda which seeks "racial purity"). Also "Our Border Brigades: The Nativist Right is Wrong," unsigned "Review and Outlook" op-ed, *Wall Street Journal*, January 27, 2004, http://www. opinionjournal.com/editorial/feature.html?id = 110004610 (accessed July 8, 2005) (opponents of illegal immigration are pursuing "the fantasy that we can or should close our borders like some isolated ancient kingdom"). Julian Simon, *The Economic Consequences of Immigration* (Cambridge: Blackwell, 1990). George W. Bush, "President Bush Proposes New Temporary Worker Program: Remarks by the President on Immigration Policy," January 7, 2004, http://www.whitehouse.gov/ news/releases/2004/01/20040107-3.html (accessed July 8, 2005) (proposing a law that would create something approaching open borders: the law would permit any foreigner offered a job to reside in America for at least six years, perhaps much longer—Bush proposed no definite time limit—"when no Americans can be found to fill the jobs"). For the libertarian advocacy of open borders, Daniel Griswold, "Reagan Embraced Free Trade and Immigration," Cato Institute publications, June 24, 2004, http://www.cato.org/pub_display.php?pub_id = 2705 (accessed August 2, 2005) (arguing that America should be "open to anyone with the will and heart to get here").

to secure those equal rights for all. In his book *Who Are We?* Samuel Huntington argues that this view of America naively assumes "that a nation can be based on only a political contract among individuals lacking any other commonality. This is the classic Enlightenment–based, civil concept of a nation. History and psychology, however, suggest that it is unlikely to be enough to sustain a nation for long." Huntington himself points to "the continuing centrality of Anglo–Protestant culture to American national identity."[3]

Some writers go further and include race, or at least "ethnicity," in their conception of national identity. Conservative publicist John O'Sullivan writes that every nation, including America, is "an ethno–cultural unit."[4] In their reasonable concern over the character and volume of recent immigration, these writers feel compelled to deny that America's founding principles define what it is to be an American.

Conservative traditionalists are wrong to believe that the Founders' natural rights idea supports the agenda of today's liberalism. But it is understandable that they hold that belief. Since the 1930s, liberals have successfully taken over the *language* of individual rights as it was understood from Washington and Jefferson to Lincoln and Coolidge. Liberals (to some extent aided by libertarians) have poured a new, alien understanding of liberty and equality into that language.

The view of equality that now holds sway is at odds with the earlier view. Most conservatives fail to acknowledge this difference. The Founders would have rejected the view that dedication to the equality principle requires mass immigration. They

---

3. Samuel P. Huntington, *Who Are We? The Challenges to America's National Identity* (New York: Simon & Schuster, 2004), 19, 30.
4. John O'Sullivan, "America's Identity Crisis," *National Review*, November 21, 1994, 37.

would very likely have supported some version of the traditionalists' restrictive immigration policy—but as an inference from the equality principle, not from its repudiation.

EQUALITY AND IMMIGRATION RESTRICTION

America is the only nation explicitly founded on the idea that all human beings are created equal in the sense that all possess the same rights to life, liberty, and the pursuit of happiness. The Declaration speaks not of the Biblical God, but of "the laws of nature and of nature's God." No one has to be Anglo–Saxon, Christian, European, or white, to be an American.

In his 1790 letter to the Hebrew Congregation in Newport, George Washington wrote:

> It is now no more that toleration is spoken of, as if it was by the indulgence of one class of people, that another enjoyed the exercise of their inherent natural rights. For happily the government of the United States, which gives to bigotry no sanction, to persecution no assistance, requires only that they who live under its protection should demean themselves as good citizens, in giving it on all occasions their effectual support.[5]

In Washington's view, all human beings, including Jews, have "inherent natural rights," one of which is the right to worship God as they choose. But people do not have an inherent natural right to conduct themselves as bad citizens. Religious conformity is not a requirement of American citizenship, nor is racial or ethnic identity—good behavior is.

---

5. Washington, "To the Hebrew Congregation in Newport, Rhode Island," (1790), in *Washington: Writings*, John Rhodehamel, ed. (New York: Library of America, 1997), 767. Capitalization, spelling, and punctuation have been modernized in quotations from the founding era.

That is why America has welcomed and assimilated immigrants far more readily than any other free country in history. Dinesh D'Souza, a naturalized American who was born in India, has remarked that it was easy for him to become an American, but that it would be impossible for a typical American to become a citizen of India. "The reason is that being Indian, like being German or Swedish or Iranian, is entirely a matter of birth and blood. You become Indian by having Indian parents."[6]

Nevertheless, the idea of liberty and equality, understood as it was by the Founders, allows restrictions on immigration, for the following reasons: "All men are created equal" means that every people, every nation, has a right to rule itself, for the same reason that every individual has a right to self-rule. If every person has the same natural right to liberty, then a people or nation can only be legitimately constituted by the free consent of every individual member. A nation is a self-selected collection of individuals who agree to live together as a political community under common laws. In the words of the Declaration of Independence, every people and every nation have the right, "among the powers of the earth," to a "separate and equal station."

A "people" is a distinct group. It does not include all of humanity. As the Declaration says, "one people" can "dissolve the political bands which have connected them with another." Once a people forms itself into a nation, no one has a right to join it without the consent of those who are already members. The reason is that equality, i.e., the equal right to liberty, means no one may be ruled without that person's consent. If a household were required to admit persons whom the homeowner did not wish to

---

6. Dinesh D'Souza, "History and Culture: Patriotism of a Higher Order," *Hoover Digest*, Fall 2002, http://www.hooverdigest.org/024/dsouza.html (accessed July 8, 2005).

admit, the fundamental principle of equality would be violated. The will of the owner would be trampled on by the will of strangers who wished to intrude. He would be ruled without his consent. The people who constitute a nation are its owners. Outsiders have no right to enter without the owners' consent.

Someone might respond, "Certainly the majority may decide how their nation is to be governed. But what if the majority's limits on immigration deny foreigners the blessings of liberty? Is not liberty a fundamental right of all mankind?" The purpose of government, the Founders would answer, is to secure the rights of the people, that is, of the members of the political society. It is not to secure the rights of persons elsewhere in the world. The Preamble of the United States Constitution says that "we the people" establish this constitution to "secure the blessings of liberty for ourselves and our posterity," not for all mankind. John Locke, the Founders' favorite philosopher when it came to first principles of government, argued that "the first and fundamental natural law, which is to govern even the legislative itself, is the preservation of the society, and (as far as will consist with the public good) of every person in it."[7]

---

7. John Locke, *Two Treatises of Government*, Peter Laslett, ed. (Cambridge: Cambridge University Press, 1988 [originally published 1690]), *Second Treatise*, sec. 134. Locke says that "The Fundamental Law of Nature being, that all, as much as may be, should be preserved" (sec. 183). This seems to mean that the government of a particular community is obliged to preserve all men throughout the world no less than its own people. But Locke does not draw that conclusion. Instead, he argues that government's active protection extends only to its own citizens, leaving other persons elsewhere in the world to shift for themselves. Of course, the prohibition against injury binds governments no less than individuals in the state of nature, so in that respect the law of nature is binding on governments in its application to all mankind. See also Donald S. Lutz, *Origins of American Constitutionalism* (Baton Rouge: Louisiana State University Press, 1988), 143. (Locke was the author most frequently

Although the primary responsibility of government is to its own citizens, that does not mean it has no duties toward others. Every individual, and every nation, has an obligation not to injure anyone, except in self–defense. Between independent nations, writes James Madison in *Federalist* 43, "the rights of humanity must in all cases be duly and mutually respected."[8] We must not harm foreigners' lives, liberty, or property. But by refusing to admit them to our community, we do not injure them or deny them their liberty. We simply leave them alone.

The natural right to liberty means that political communities, like homeowners, are free to exclude would-be entrants. It also means that individuals are free to emigrate. Pennsylvania's 1776 Declaration of Rights states: "all men have a natural inherent right to emigrate from one state to another that will receive them, or to form a new state in vacant countries, or in such countries as they can purchase, whenever they think that thereby they may promote their own happiness." The right of a nation to exclude immigrants is implied when Pennsylvania adds that the right to emigrate to another state is only "to another *that will receive them.*"

Jefferson had already tied the right to emigrate to the fundamental natural right to liberty in his widely read *A Summary View of the Rights of British America* (1774): there is "a right which nature has given to all men, of departing from the country in which chance, not choice, has placed them, of going in quest of new habitations, and of

---

cited in published political writings during the quarrel with Britain in the 1760s and 1770s, when first principles of government were the leading concerns).

8. Alexander Hamilton, James Madison, and John Jay, *The Federalist Papers*, No. 43 (Madison), introduction and notes by Charles R. Kesler, Clinton Rossiter, ed. (New York: Signet Classic, 2003), 277.

there establishing new societies, under such laws and regulations as to them shall seem most likely to promote public happiness."[9]

THE PROBLEM OF REPUBLICAN GOVERNMENT

The equality principle may *permit* a people to decide which outsiders should be admitted and which excluded. But just because they have that right, should they exercise it? If so, in what way and for what ends? To answer that question, let us look more closely at what the equality principle means.

The Declaration of Independence states two criteria of just government. First, the purpose of government is to secure the citizens' right to liberty and their other natural rights. Second, government must derive its just powers from the consent of the governed. To deny the people the right of self–government, *or* to deny some of them their equal rights to life and liberty, would fail to satisfy one of the two fundamental criteria of the founding. It would be to assert in effect that some men are so superior to others that they may rule them as masters rule their slaves, without the slaves' consent.

The ten years after independence in 1776 taught Americans the hard lesson that these two requirements of just government are not necessarily in harmony. *Consent* (or majority rule) does not always lead to security of *rights*. The people may err. The majority, as James Madison wrote in *Federalist* 10, may become a faction and deprive the minority of its just rights.

A long recession after the Revolutionary War led to increasingly radical measures, including the intentional inflation of the currency by several state governments in order

---

9. Jefferson, "Summary View" (1774), in *Jefferson: Writings*, Merrill D. Peterson, ed. (New York: Library of America, 1984), 105.

to relieve debtors. Rhode Island passed laws requiring merchants to accept almost worthless currency for their goods. Business came to a standstill. Mobs attacked those who refused to sell their goods at a loss.

The argument of *The Federalist* is that the right kind of government structure can help prevent this sort of majority faction. Madison and the Constitution's framers placed much of their trust in a government conducted by elected representatives, spread out over a large country; a two–house legislature; a strong one–person executive; and a judiciary with lifetime appointments. But the Founders knew that constitutional devices are not enough.

In his First Inaugural Address, Jefferson pointed to the tension within the Declaration by speaking of "this sacred principle, that though the will of the majority is in all cases to prevail, that will, to be rightful, must be reasonable; that the minority possess their equal rights, which equal laws must protect, and to violate which would be oppression." Jefferson then went on to praise the religious and moral convictions of Americans, because he knew that they helped to make the will of the people reasonable and therefore rightful. In Query 18 of his *Notes on Virginia*, Jefferson had written that the "only firm basis" of the liberties of a nation is "a conviction in the minds of the people that these liberties are of the gift of God."[10] Jefferson knew that a free people must have not only sensible political institutions to discourage oppression, but also the right character and beliefs, if a regime of liberty is to be sustained. That is also why he, along with John Adams and George Washington, paid so much attention to public education.

In this light it becomes apparent that although all human beings have a *right* to be free, not all have the immediate

---

10. Jefferson, "First Inaugural Address" (1801), *Writings*, Peterson, ed., 492-494. *Notes on the State of Virginia* (1787), 289.

capacity to be free. It depends on their character and their beliefs.

THE FOUNDERS' IMMIGRATION POLICY

For this reason—namely, the importance for good citizenship of religion, education, and sound moral character—the Founders' immigration policy had two parts. In the first place, many immigrants were welcomed with remarkable liberality. Europeans who came to America became citizens with little difficulty. Washington expressed the common view when he wrote, "The bosom of America is open to receive not only the opulent and respectable stranger, but the oppressed and persecuted of all nations and religions."[11] America's early openness to non–Protestant citizens is evident in the generous 1774 letter from the Continental Congress inviting the Catholic inhabitants of Quebec "to unite with us in one social compact, formed on the generous principles of equal liberty, and cemented by such an exchange of beneficial and endearing offices as to render it perpetual." On the sensitive matter of religion, Congress wrote, "We are too well acquainted with the liberality of sentiment distinguishing your nation to imagine, that difference of religion will prejudice you against a hearty amity with us. You know that the transcendent nature of freedom elevates those who unite in her cause above all such low–minded infirmities."[12] Here is the beginning of America's long and honorable tradition of welcoming as equal citizens more

11. "Washington to the Members of the Volunteer Association of Ireland," December 2, 1783, in *Writings of George Washington*, John C. Fitzpatrick, ed. (Washington: Government Printing Office, 1931-44), 27:254.
12. "Appeal to the Inhabitants of Quebec," in *American Political Writing during the Founding Era, 1760-1805*, Charles S. Hyneman and Donald S. Lutz, eds. (Indianapolis: Liberty Press, 1983), 1:235-238.

voluntary immigrants than any nation in history. However, sentiments like these did not lead the Founders to favor unlimited immigration. Immigrants of the wrong sort and in the wrong quantity would threaten liberty. That reflection leads to the second part of their immigration policy.

The rest of the sentence quoted from Washington above (after he affirms America's openness to immigrants "of all nations and religions") reads: "whom we shall welcome to a participation of all our rights and privileges, *if by decency and propriety of conduct they appear to merit the enjoyment*" (my emphasis).[13] Good character was understood as a reasonable condition of citizenship.

The nation's first naturalization law therefore required "proof" that the applicant be "a person of good character." Every applicant also had to take "the oath or affirmation prescribed by law to support the Constitution of the United States."[14]

John Adams warned a European who was considering relocating to America: "All the world knows that my country is open to strangers"; however, only those "who love liberty, innocence [i.e., not harming others], and industry are sure of an easy, comfortable life."[15]

Washington's hope that America might become an "asylum to the *virtuous* and persecuted part of mankind, to whatever nation they may belong" led him to go out of his way to encourage Dutch Mennonites to settle in America. The Dutch were "sober, industrious, and virtuous," and "friends

---

13. "Washington to the Members of the Volunteer Association of Ireland," *Writings*, Fitzpatrick, ed., 27:254.
14. Naturalization Act, March 26, 1790, *Documentary History of the First Federal Congress*, vol. 6, Charlene B. Bickford et al., eds. (Baltimore: Johns Hopkins University Press, 1986), 1516.
15. Adams to John Wooddrop, February 3, 1786, in *Papers of Thomas Jefferson*, Julian P. Boyd et al. eds. (Princeton: Princeton University Press, 1950–), 13:432.

to the rights of mankind," he wrote to a Dutch preacher recently arrived in New York; they would therefore be "a valuable acquisition to our infant settlements."[16]

Washington's consistent concern with immigrant character and beliefs reflects his statesmanlike focus on citizenship, which in turn reflects his overriding concern with the preservation of freedom. In sharp contrast, many today speak of immigration as if it were merely an economic question, as if the willingness to work for low wages were a sufficient reason to approve of immigration.

The first naturalization law of 1790 limited naturalization to "any alien being a free white person, who shall have resided," etc.[17] Today such racial language is taken to be an expression of irrational bigotry in contradiction to the Founders' supposed belief that all men are born equally free. But there are other, better explanations of the "free white" clause.

We have already noted that the Founders made a distinction that we are not accustomed to make, between the right to freedom and the right to be a citizen. It was not inconsistent, therefore, to oppose black slavery and also to oppose black citizenship. If citizenship is a matter of mutual consent, then a free person can become a citizen of any nation that will have him. But he has no right to demand membership in a particular society as a matter of natural right.

Being white was obviously a racial difference, but the racial distinction, in the context of early American history, also pointed to a civilizational difference. The authors of the 1790 act were obviously using "white" as a rough equivalent of "European," in contrast to blacks and Indians.

---

16. Washington, Letter to Rev. Francis Vanderkemp, May 28, 1788, *Writings*, Fitzpatrick, ed., 29:504–505 (emphasis added).

17. Naturalization Act, in *Documentary History*, vol. 6, Bickford, ed., 1516.

Europe was the realm of what we now call Western civilization. The words quoted in the previous pages from Washington and other Founders show that they were thinking of civilization, not whiteness, when they reflected on the positive qualities that at least some European immigrants would bring with them to America. Europeans as a group shared with Americans a heritage of morality, religion, and respect for reason that made them, in the Founders' view, the most likely candidates for successful assimilation into democratic citizenship. Washington wrote, with a view to these qualities:

> The foundation of our empire was not laid in the gloomy age of ignorance and superstition, but at an epoch when the rights of mankind were better understood and more clearly defined than at any former period;...the free cultivation of letters, the unbounded extension of commerce, the progressive refinement of manners, the growing liberality of sentiment, and above all, the pure and benign light of revelation, have had a meliorating influence on mankind and increased the blessings of society.[18]

As Washington indicates in his reference to "the benign light of revelation," the legal preference for "white" immigrants was at the same time a de facto preference for Christians, for in those days Christianity was mostly limited to Europeans, and most Europeans were Christians. It is true that the founding principles required government to secure the natural right to the free exercise of religion for worshipers of all faiths. Christianity (or any other religion) may nevertheless be favored by government through its immigration policy without violating anyone's religious liberty. In the

---

18. Washington, "Circular to the States" (1783), *Writings*, Rhodehamel, ed., 517.

founding era and through most of American history, Christianity was widely regarded as the best religious foundation for free institutions. This is probably what Washington meant by "the pure and benign light of revelation." An 1810 Massachusetts Supreme Court decision expressed the early American consensus, arguing that Protestant Christianity contains

> a system of morals adopted to man, in all possible ranks and conditions, situations and circumstances, by conforming to which he would be meliorated and improved in all the relations of human life;...and tending, by its effects, to make every man submitting to its influence, a better husband, parent, child, neighbor, citizen, and magistrate.[19]

It is a notorious fact that many religious sects in the world today do not make their adherents "a better husband, parent, child, neighbor, citizen, and magistrate." Instead, their teachings mandate hatred and sometimes murder of one's fellow citizens, if those citizens hold the wrong religious opinions. These religions sometimes promote the despotic subordination of women to men, including polygamy. In the Founders' view, a nation has both the right and the duty to prefer immigrants whose religions are friendly toward, and compatible with, the elementary conditions of freedom and the preservation of the nation.[20]

---

19. Barnes v. First Parish in Falmouth, 6 Mass. 401 (1810), opinion of Chief Justice Theophilus Parsons for the Supreme Judicial Court of Massachusetts, in *Religious Freedom: History, Cases, and Other Materials on the Interaction of Religion and Government*, John T. Noonan and Edward McGlynn Gaffney, eds. (New York: Foundation Press, 2001), 224. See also Jefferson's praise of Christianity as a "benign religion" in his First Inaugural Address (1801), in *Jefferson: Writings*, Peterson, ed., 494.
20. For a recent defense of the view that government should concern itself with the content of the religious convictions of citizens of a constitutional democracy, see Richard Garnett, "Assimilation, Toleration, and

An additional reason for promoting European immigration was that national unity is more likely among people who are similar in race, customs, and religion. In *Federalist 2*, John Jay wrote:

> Providence has been pleased to give this one connected country to one united people, a people descended from the same ancestors, speaking the same language, professing the same religion, attached to the same principles of government, very similar in their manners and customs.[21]

Jay was alluding to the natural preference of human beings to associate with people of their own kind. The preference for one's own—whether in ancestry, religion, manners, morals, or political principles—is not noble, but it is also not evil, as long as it does not interfere with the duty to respect the equal rights of all. That preference may prove useful or even indispensable if it leads to a citizen body

---

the State's Interest in the Development of Religious Doctrine," *UCLA Law Review* 51 (2004): 1–59. Garnett argues that "the health of civil society depends crucially on the formation, development, and training of capable, decent, other–regarding persons who are concerned with and motivated by the common good....[A] democratic political community [cannot] perpetuate itself without attending carefully to the dispositions of its citizens....[T]he liberal state is not and cannot be indifferent to the substantive content of the messages and teachings that shape those who would be liberal citizens. If religious doctrine plays a role in the formation of citizens, then it can only be of interest to liberal governments" (54–55). John Locke, in his *Letter on Toleration*, famously argues that government is required to tolerate all religiously motivated beliefs, worship, and actions. But Locke also argues, in a passage that is not so widely noted, that a religion loses its right to be tolerated if its teachings oppose minimal standards of moral rectitude and the duty to obey government: "no doctrines adverse and contrary to human society, or to the good morals that are necessary to the preservation of civil society, are to be tolerated by the magistrate." Locke, *Epistola de Tolerantia* (Goudae: Apud Justum Ab Hoeve, 1689), 73 (my translation).

21. *The Federalist Papers,* No. 2 (John Jay), 32.

that is more likely to respect the rights of all and to support a political regime that effectively secures those rights. We have already noted that the right to liberty includes liberty of association, and therefore the right to include or exclude would–be immigrants. Benjamin Franklin bluntly stated that he preferred English immigrants because other Europeans "are generally of what we call a swarthy complexion; as are the Germans also, the Saxons alone excepted." Franklin excused his all–too–human feelings with this remark: "But perhaps I am partial to the complexion of my country, for such kind of partiality is natural to mankind."[22]

Finally, the "free white" clause in the naturalization law was specifically linked to a concern shared by most Americans in the founding era about citizenship for free blacks. Noah Pickus writes:

> Scholars have not found any debate over the free white clause because they have been looking in the wrong place—in the debates over naturalization rather than the controversy over emancipation. What emerges from such a picture is not simply a matter of political compromise, a preference for a shared European heritage, or an unconflicted ideology of racism. Rather, these debates reveal how many leaders agonized over the tension between blacks' natural right to freedom and prudential concerns about an integrated nation. The free white clause terminology was consistent in the minds of those who opposed slavery with ensuring a cohesive community.

In spite of this troubling "free white" clause, nothing in the Founders' principles had to be changed for blacks to be admitted to full citizenship, as they were after the Civil War. Considerations of the sort that we have just discussed

---

22. Franklin, "Observations Concerning the Increase of Mankind, Peopling of Countries, etc." (1751), in *Franklin: Writings*, J. A. Leo Lemay, ed. (New York: Library of America, 1987), 374.

were swept away by that tremendous event. The Fourteenth Amendment, passed in its immediate wake, granted citizenship to everyone born in America who is "subject to the jurisdiction" of American law, i.e., does not owe allegiance to any other nation.[23]

The Founders' preference for European immigrants was therefore perfectly compatible with the equality principle of the founding, according to which the social compact is formed by a voluntary agreement between the individual and the rest of the citizens for the securing of the natural rights of all the compacting members.

Besides being concerned about the *character* of immigrants, the Founders also noted the problem created when *too many* of them come at one time.

Long before independence, Franklin had worried that Pennsylvania Germans, "by herding together," were establishing "their language and manners to the exclusion of ours."[24] Over forty years later, in a letter to his vice president, Washington wrote that "the policy or advantage of

---

23. On the debate over black citizenship in the early republic, see Thomas G. West, *Vindicating the Founders: Race, Sex, Class, and Justice in the Origins of America* (Lanham: Rowman & Littlefield, 1997), 25–28. Madison, Memorandum on an African Colony for Freed Slaves (1789), in *The Founders' Constitution*, Philip B. Kurland and Ralph Lerner, eds. (Chicago: University of Chicago Press, 1987), 1:552. Jefferson, Letter to Bancroft, Jan. 26, 1788, *Papers*, 14:492. Leon F. Litwack, *North of Slavery: The Negro in the Free States, 1790–1860* (Chicago: University of Chicago Press, 1961), 94 (the Pennsylvania report). Frederick Douglass, "What Are the Colored People Doing for Themselves?" (1848), in Herbert J. Storing, ed., *What Country Have I? Political Writings by Black Americans* (New York: St. Martin's, 1970), 45–46. Noah Pickus is one of the few scholars who sees the connection between the "free white person" clause of the 1794 Naturalization Act and this widespread doubt about the quality of free blacks as citizens—although he is not very sympathetic toward that doubt. See Noah Pickus, *True Faith and Allegiance: Immigration and American Civic Nationalism* (Princeton: Princeton University Press, 2005), chapter 3 (on "The Free White Clause of 1790"), 52–53.
24. Franklin, "Observation," *Writings*, 374.

[immigration] taking place in a body (I mean the settling of them in a body) may be much questioned; for, by so doing, they retain the language, habits, and principles (good or bad) which they bring with them. Whereas by an intermixture with our people, they, or their descendants, get assimilated to our customs, measures, and laws: in a word, soon become one people."[25]

In Query 8 of his *Notes on Virginia*, Jefferson summarized nicely the Founders' caution concerning unlimited immigration. He wrote that the principles of American government, "more peculiar than those of any other in the universe," are "a composition of the freest principles of the English constitution, with others derived from natural right and natural reason." That is, America's principles are liberty and equality, combined with *only* that part of the British tradition which is fully compatible with liberty and equality. Maintaining American principles, Jefferson thought, was crucial to the survival of liberty.

Jefferson knew that "the greatest number of emigrants" would come from "absolute monarchies," just as today most come from countries ruled undemocratically or with minimal protection of individual rights. "They will bring with them," he wrote, "the principles of the governments they leave, imbibed in their early youth; or, if able to throw them off, it will be in exchange for an unbounded licentiousness." The result: "In proportion to their numbers, they will share with us the legislation. They will infuse into it their spirit, warp and bias its direction."[26]

Jefferson was not saying that America is primarily an ethnic or cultural unit, as traditionalists now say. Nor did he believe that "all men are created equal" means open

---

25. Washington to the Vice President (Adams), November 15, 1794, *Writings*, Fitzpatrick, ed., 34:23.
26. Jefferson, *Notes on the State of Virginia*, Query 8, *Writings*, 211.

borders, as liberals and libertarians claim. It is the equality principle itself that calls for limits on immigration, if the number or character of the immigrants threatens to change America's laws in such a way that they would no longer secure the natural rights of the people by means of government by consent of the governed.[27]

IMPLICATIONS FOR TODAY: THE QUESTION OF CHARACTER

Suppose that at the request of Mexico and the Central American nations, Congress passed a law expanding America's southern border to Columbia. Or suppose ten or twenty Asian and African countries were admitted as new states of the United States, with full voting and citizenship rights. No one would deny that America would become overnight a dramatically different country. The habits and convictions of the new population would immediately become a dominant factor in the nation's counsels.

Since 1965, when today's immigration policy began, America has effectively put a modified version of this plan into place, but without redrawing its borders. In huge numbers, America has admitted people from areas of the world

---

27. A fuller account of the Founders' approach to immigration can be found in chapter 7 of West, *Vindicating the Founders*. The first part of the present essay is based on that chapter. John Marini's chapter in the present volume argues that Progressive era racial theory, not the Founders' legitimate concern for the conditions of citizenship, was used to justify the restrictive Immigration Act of 1924. Whatever may have been the intentions of those who passed that law, the Founders' theory of free government, which was not grounded on any theory of racial supremacy, could have led in 1924 to a similar law, but for different reasons. There was a need to restrict the massive flow of immigration that had already created tremendous obstacles to assimilation and which, as we will see later in this chapter, would soon create an even more serious challenge to the perpetuation of the American regime itself.

where political liberty in the Founders' sense does not exist and, for the most part, has never existed—to say nothing of moral restraint, manly vigilance, and a proper understanding of human equality.

There is a lively contemporary debate over the character of these recent immigrants. Immigration restrictionists like Peter Brimelow argue that their tendency toward licentious conduct can be seen especially in the area of crime. Brimelow writes that although the Italian Mafia has been in decline in recent years, "There are several new 'mafias,' each with its own specialties: Colombians (cocaine); Mexicans (marijuana, auto theft, alien smuggling); Hong Kong Chinese (heroin, alien smuggling); South Koreans (prostitution)....'The Russians are just as crazy as the Jamaican drug gangs,' a Ukrainian–speaking New York detective [said]; 'They won't hesitate to go after a cop's family'." Brimelow notes further that "U.S. law enforcement officials estimate an incredible *75 percent* of the 100,000 Nigerians now in the United States are involved in 'an impressive and innovative variety of fraud schemes'." including "immigration and citizenship fraud; bank and credit card fraud; welfare fraud; insurance fraud; heroin." The MS 13 gang, composed of recent immigrants from El Salvador, has an estimated 8,000 to 10,000 members. *Newsweek* calls it the "fastest growing, most violent...of the nation's street gangs"; it is "the most dangerous gang in America."[28]

28. Peter Brimelow, *Alien Nation: Common Sense about America's Immigration Disaster* (New York: Random House, 1995), 185–186. In support of Brimelow: Lawrence Auster, *The Path to National Suicide: An Essay on Immigration and Multiculturalism* (Monterrey, Va.: American Immigration Control Foundation, 1994); Patrick J. Buchanan, *The Death of the West: How Dying Populations and Immigrant Invasions Imperil Our Country and Civilization* (New York: Thomas Dunne Books, 2002); Victor Davis Hanson, *Mexifornia: A State of Becoming* (San Francisco: Encounter Books, 2003); Huntington, *Who Are We?*; Heather Mac Donald, "The Illegal-Alien Crime Wave," CityJournal,Winter 2004, http://www.city-journal.org/html/14_

Other problems abound among Hispanic immigrants. According to the U.S. Census Bureau's 2000 Current Population Survey, 31 percent of Mexican immigrant households, but only 15 percent of native households, were using one or more of the major federal welfare programs in 1999.[29] In a 1995 National Highway Traffic Safety Administration study, "21 percent of those arrested for impaired driving [i.e., driving under the influence of alcohol and other drugs] nationally were Hispanic, while at the time of the study Hispanics accounted for only 9 percent of the population." In the same publication, recent immigrants were reported to be particularly dangerous drivers. In its annual study of leading causes of death, the U.S. Centers for Disease Control found that twice as many Hispanics as non–Hispanics died of accidents in 2002.[30]

1_the_illegal_alien.html (accessed July 8, 2005); Mac Donald, "The Immigrant Gang Plague," City Journal, Summer 2004, http://www.city-journal.org/html/14_3_immigrant_gang.html (accessed July 8, 2005); Michelle Malkin, Invasion: How America Still Welcomes Terrorists, Criminals, and Other Foreign Menaces to Our Shores (Washington: Regnery, 2002). Arian Campo–Flores, "The Most Dangerous Gang in America," Newsweek, March 28, 2005, http://www.msnbc.msn.com/id/7244879/site/newsweek/ (accessed September 20, 2006) (on the MS 13 gang).

29. Welfare rates: Steven A. Camerota, "Immigration from Mexico: Assessing the Impact on the United States," Center for Immigration Studies, July 2001, http://www.cis.org/articles/2001/mexico/mexico.pdf (accessed October 14, 2005) (based on the March 2000 Current Population Survey (CPS) collected by the Census Bureau, 39).

30. Drunk–driving and accident death rates: "Highway Safety Needs of U.S. Hispanic Communities: Issues and Strategies," National Highway Traffic Safety Administration, U.S. Department of Transportation, September 1995, DOT HS 808 373, http://www.nhtsa.dot.gov/people/injury/research/pub/hispanic.pdf, 18, 37 (accessed April 1, 2006). Robert N. Anderson et al., "Deaths: Leading Causes for 2002," National Vital Statistics Reports, vol. 53, no. 17, Hyattsville, Maryland: National Center for Health Statistics, 2005, Table F, http://www.cdc.gov/nchs/data/nvsr/nvsr53/nvsr53_17.pdf (accessed April 1, 2006).

The *Washington Post* reported that "Attorney General William P. Barr said nearly one–third of the first 6,000 riot suspects arrested and processed through the court system [during the Los Angeles riots of 1992] were illegal aliens." Over one–fourth of federal prisoners are non–citizens, and most of these non–citizens are Hispanic. The National Center on Institutions and Alternatives, using state–level data from 1997, found that Hispanics are imprisoned three times as often as whites. The U.S. National Center for Health Statistics reported that in 2003, almost three times as many Hispanics as whites died of homicide.[31]

According to the U.S. Centers for Disease Control, 46.4 percent of births to Hispanic women took place outside of marriage in 2004, compared with 24.5 percent for non–Hispanic whites. That is, the Hispanic nonmarital birth rate is almost double the white rate. In the general population, children born to single mothers are the leading source of the criminal class. They are far more likely than other children to commit crimes, join gangs, abuse alcohol and drugs, perform poorly in school, become unemployed, and suffer child abuse, as I show in *Vindicating the Founders.*[32]

---

31. Brimelow, *Alien Nation*, 182 (prison population). Brimelow, "Time to Rethink Immigration?" *National Review*, June 22, 1992, Postscript, http://vdare.com/pb/time_to_rethink2.htm, (accessed April 1, 2006) (quoting the *Washington Post* quoting Attorney General Barr). Steve Sailer, "Mapping the Unmentionable: Race and Crime," February 13, 2005, http://www.vdare.com/sailer/050213_mapping.htm (accessed October 14, 2005) (crime rates). Donna L. Hoyert et al., Deaths: Final data for 2003. U.S. National Center for Health Statistics, Health E-Stats, January 19, 2006, Table 3, http://www.cdc.gov/nchs/data/hestat/finaldeaths03_tables.pdf (accessed April 1, 2006) (homicide death rates).
32. Brady E. Hamilton et al., "Preliminary Births for 2004," Health E-stats, Hyattsville, MD: National Center for Health Statistics, October 28, 2005, Table 1, http://www.cdc.gov/nchs/data/hesta/prelimbirth04_tables.pdf (accessed April 1, 2006). *Vindicating the Founders*, chapter 4, "Women and the Family."

All of this evidence suggests that Jefferson was right when he predicted that immigrants accustomed to living under governments that do not protect individual rights and do not encourage habits of self–restraint would be less likely to be good citizens.

Those on the pro–immigration side of the debate respond by pointing out that many immigrants have become and continue to become hard–working, decent citizens—often more hard-working and decent than natives. William Bennett quotes a math teacher saying that immigrants are "why I love teaching in Brooklyn. They have a drive in them that we no longer seem to have." Other such anecdotes abound.[33] The question, however, is not whether immigrants today make superior citizens in some individual cases. The question is whether these immigrants as a whole are behaving themselves as well as the rest of America. As the evidence shows, they are not.

THE POLITICAL CONSEQUENCES OF THE
1880–1914 IMMIGRANT WAVE

To get some perspective on today's immigration, recall what happened during and after the last great immigration wave—the one from Southern and Eastern Europe between 1880 and 1914. For the next three or four generations, the offspring of these immigrants voted overwhelmingly against policies based on what Jefferson called "the freest principles

---

33. William J. Bennett, "Revolt against God: America's Spiritual Despair," *Policy Review*, Winter 1994, 19. Bennett, "A Manifesto for Immigration," *Wall Street Journal*, February 29, 1996, A14. In support of Bennett: Francis Fukuyama, "Immigrants and Family Values," *Commentary*, May 1993, 26–32; Tamar Jacoby, *Reinventing the Melting Pot* (New York: Basic Books, 2004) (arguing that the melting pot still works, and that today's immigration is not a significant problem).

of the English constitution, with others derived from natural right and natural reason." Instead of favoring Jeffersonian, limited, decentralized, constitutional government devoted to securing individual liberty and property rights, a large majority of these voters have supported the construction, step by step, of the centralized and bureaucratized modern administrative state. The Democratic Party was swept into power in the 1930s in large measure by the votes of these immigrants. Historian Samuel Lubell tells the story:

> [According to a 1910 report to Congress on immigration,] a majority of the children in the schools of thirty–seven of the nation's leading cities had foreign–born fathers. In cities like...Duluth, New York, and Chicago more than two out of every three school children were the sons and daughters of immigrants. Viewed in today's perspective, it is clear that those figures forecast a major political up-heaval some time between 1930 and 1940. By then all of these children, plus baby brothers and sisters not enrolled in school, would have grown to voting age. Massed as they were in the states commanding the largest electoral vote, their sheer numbers would topple any prevailing political balance....[T]he big–city masses furnished the votes which re–elected Roosevelt again and again—and, in the process, ended the traditional Republican majority in this country.[34]

According to political scientist Norman Nie, many older-stock Americans continued to vote Republican as much as ever:

> [T]he nature of partisan attachment—in particular the habitual and unchanging character of party identification for the majority of citizens—was not significantly differ-ent in the 1920s and 1930s from what it is today. The

---

34. Samuel Lubell, *The Future of American Politics* , 3rd ed. (New York: Harper Colophon, 1965), 43-44.

shift to a Democratic majority occurred largely through the entry of new groups into the active electorate between 1920 and 1936. These new entrants consisted of young voters entering the electorate and older (largely immigrant or second generation) Americans voting for the first time. The conversion of long–time Republicans played a far less significant role.[35]

Of course, many of these new Democratic voters were offspring of older American groups. Nevertheless, Nie concludes, "the immigrants and their children are credited with a decisive role in the major political realignment of the [Franklin] Roosevelt era."[36]

The grandchildren and great–grandchildren of these earlier immigrants, along with more recent immigrants from the Caribbean and Latin America, voted in large majorities for the consolidation and expansion of the administrative state since the 1960s. Nie reports that as late as 1967, opinion surveys found that descendants of Southern and Eastern Europeans were almost 20 percent more likely than other Americans to approve of government provision of medical care, employment, and housing.[37]

A 1989–90 survey analyzed by political scientist Rodolfo de la Garza found that Latinos (especially Mexican and Puerto Rican Americans) are much more supportive than European–Americans of racial preferences for jobs and college admissions, and of government provision of jobs, housing, and minimum income. For example, writes de la Garza, "Where the majority of Puerto Rican and Mexican respondents saw a need for increased government expenditure for

35. Norman H. Nie et al., *The Changing American Voter*, enlarged ed. (Cambridge: Harvard University Press, 1979), 75.
36. Norman H. Nie et al., "Political Attitudes among American Ethnics," in Andrew M. Greeley, *Ethnicity in the United States: A Preliminary Reconnaissance* (New York: John Wiley, 1974), 187.
37. Ibid., 192.

programs to assist blacks, the majority of Cubans and Anglos did not." Differences of opinion on merit–based hiring and college admissions are dramatic. According to de la Garza, over 52 percent of European– and Cuban–Americans favor merit as the sole basis of jobs and college admissions, while only 29 percent of Mexicans and 25 percent of Puerto Ricans hold the same opinion. Similarly, Asians voted solidly liberal in the 2000 and 2004 presidential elections.[38]

Cuban–Americans are an exception to Jefferson's general rule that immigrants from despotic nations are likely to hold political views at odds with the Founders' understanding of republican government. The same may also be said of Vietnamese. In a 2004 pre–election poll sponsored by New California Media, Vietnamese–Americans preferred Republican Bush over Democrat Kerry by a margin of 71 to 11 percent. (I explain further below why I take the preference for today's Democratic Party to be a sign of an underlying preference for the administrative state). Other Asians (except Filipinos, who favored Bush 56 to 30 percent) were either

---

38. Rodolfo O. de la Garza et al., *Latino Voices: Mexican, Puerto Rican, and Cuban Perspectives on American Politics* (Boulder: Westview Press, 1992), 85–86 (polling data on Hispanic attitudes toward government's role in job provision, housing provision, and assuring minimum income), 90 (programs to assist blacks), 110 (percentages favoring strictly merit). In the 2004 exit poll conducted jointly by the major American media, Asian Americans favored Democrat Kerry over Republican Bush by a 56–44 percent margin: http://www.cnn.com/ELECTION/2004/pages/results/states/US/P/00/epolls.0.html (accessed Sept. 5, 2006). In the 2000 Voter News Service Exit Poll, 55 percent of Asians voted for Gore, 41 percent for Bush. (Reported in New California Media, National Survey of Asian and Pacific Islander Likely Voters in the United States, September 14, 2004, conducted by Bendixen & Associates and The Tarrance Group, http://news.newamericamedia.org (accessed Sept. 5, 2006). Less believable is the 75 percent Kerry vote reported in *The Asian American Vote 2004: A Report on the Multilingual Exit Poll in the 2004 Presidential Election*, conducted by the Asian American Legal Defense and Education Fund. This survey was limited to a small number of cities, most of them strongly Democratic.

more evenly divided between the Republican and Democratic candidate for president, or else were overwhelmingly Democratic in their preference. The explanation generally given for the Cuban and Vietnamese exception to the general voting pattern of immigrants, writes reporter Andrew Lam, is that "Republicans are perceived as being strong against terrorism and, more important, communism. The majority of the Vietnamese population is foreign born who were once refugees fleeing communism, and many still remember what it was like to live under dictatorship."[39] But Vietnamese make up only a small portion of the overall Asian population.

From a political standpoint, then, just as in the 1930s and 1960s, so also today, continued rapid immigration will strengthen the modern administrative state and further erode the influence of America's founding principles on American political life. Many Democrats today, at any rate, are unabashed enthusiasts for almost unlimited immigration, while Republicans are deeply divided on that question.

THE CONFLICT BETWEEN THE KIND OF GOVERNMENT FAVORED BY IMMIGRANTS AND THE PRINCIPLES OF CONSTITUTIONAL GOVERNMENT

From the Founders' point of view, these voting patterns are troubling. The theoretical basis of the welfare state was conceived in direct opposition to Jefferson and the founding, as Progressive era writers made explicit. Woodrow Wilson's and Franklin Roosevelt's understanding of the purpose of

---

39. National Survey of Asian and Pacific Islander Likely Voters, September 14, 2004. Andrew Lam, "Vietnamese Americans Back President Bush —But For How Long?" *Berkeley Daily Planet*, October 5, 2004, http:// www.berkeleydailyplanet.com (accessed Sept. 5, 2006).

politics was derived from these writers. Roosevelt's plan—
only a fraction of which he was able to implement during
the 1930s and 1940s—was to use the power of government
to guarantee to every citizen a comfortable living, including appropriate recreation, as a fundamental right. In other
words, property was no longer viewed as something that
each family was expected to produce through its own efforts, except in cases of dire necessity. Instead, property
would be viewed as a public trust. Government would re-
distribute it or mandate its proper use so that all would
share in the common wealth.[40]

In the 1960s and 1970s, after the nation had grown more
wealthy, government began to implement Roosevelt's plan
much more thoroughly than had been possible when FDR
was in office. This effort has led to substantial curbs on the
rights of individuals as the Founders conceived them. In the
name of protecting women, minorities, and the poor, government curtailed speech, broadcasting, and publications
through broadcast regulation, campaign finance regulation,
labor law regulations, and harassment regulation.[41] The

---

40. On the transformation of American politics accomplished by Roos-
evelt and 1960s liberalism, see John Marini, *The Politics of Budget
Control: Congress, the Presidency, and the Growth of the Administrative
State* (Washington: Crane Russak, 1992), 88–107; Edward J. Erler, *The
American Polity: Essays on the Theory and Practice of American Govern-
ment* (New York: Crane Russak, 1991), 91–116; Sidney M. Milkis, *The
President and the Parties: The Transformation of the American Party Sys-
tem Since the New Deal* (New York: Oxford, 1993); Tiffany Jones Miller,
"Transforming Formal Freedom into Effective Freedom: John Dewey, the
New Deal, and the Great Society," in *Modern America and the Legacy of
the Founding*, Ronald J. Pestritto and Thomas G. West, eds. (Lanham:
Lexington Books, 2006). On Roosevelt's link to Progressive intellectuals,
Robert Eden, "On the Origins of the Regime of Pragmatic Liberalism:
John Dewey, Adolf A. Berle, and FDR's Commonwealth Club Address of
1932," *Studies in American Political Development*, 7 (1993): 74–150.
41. Thomas G. West, "Freedom of Speech in the American Founding and
in Modern Liberalism," in *Freedom of Speech*, Ellen Frankel Paul, Fred D.

right to use one's property was hemmed in by extensive licensing requirements, regulatory micromanagement, increasingly restrictive zoning laws, high taxes, and wetlands and endangered species regulation. Eventually, government issued sweeping mandates to businesses to provide services for those deemed deserving by government, such as the Americans with Disabilities Act of 1990 and the requirement that hospitals provide free medical care for anyone who shows up who claims to be unable to pay.[42]

Some scholars have noted (but most have not) the huge gulf between the Founders' Declaration–of–Independence belief in equality and the kind of equality sought by welfare-state liberalism. When men like John Dewey and Herbert Croly laid out the theoretical grounds for today's welfare state early in the twentieth century, they explicitly and repeatedly attacked the Founders and the political theory of the Declaration and the Constitution. Dewey rejected limited government based on natural rights as a social order "established by an unplanned and external convergence of the actions of separate individuals, each of whom is bent on personal private advantage." He wanted to replace the limited, constitutional government established by the Founders with unlimited government based on the idea of an evolving idea of liberty and "organized social planning." According to Dewey, "evil...lay in the assertion by earlier liberalism [that is, by the American Founders] of the immutable and

Miller, Jr., and Jeffrey Paul, eds. (New York: Cambridge University Press, 2004), 310–384.

42. One of the most honest presentations by a liberal of the liberal hostility to property rights outlined in this paragraph is by Justice William Brennan, "To the Text and Teaching Symposium," Georgetown University, October 15, 1985, in Edwin Meese et al., *The Great Debate: Interpreting Our Written Constitution* (Washington: The Federalist Society, 1986), 19. Jennifer Nedelsky is also very blunt in *Private Property and the Limits of American Constitutionalism: The Madisonian Framework and Its Limits* (Chicago: University of Chicago Press, 1990).

eternal character of their ideas." The "evil" in question is the Founders' idea of individual rights, including private property rights. In Dewey's mind, this "evil" stands in the way of modern liberalism, which is compelled to violate the individual speech rights or property rights of some citizens in order to favor other citizens deemed disadvantaged.[43]

This is the kind of government that the children and descendants of post–1880 immigrants have been voting for in large majorities over the past century. One explanation may be that it is the kind of government that they were familiar with in the nations from which they emigrated. Despotisms do not operate by rule of laws that treat all citizens alike. They govern in the interests of those in the government and their friends and clients. This leads their subjects to have a cynical view of government, to expect nothing except self-interest on the part of government officials. Those who live under such governments are compelled to seek out a patron in or connected with the government—someone to help them, their clients, to get favors or avoid the arbitrary oppression suffered by those who do not have such

---

43. John Dewey, *Liberalism and Social Action* (New York: Perigree, Putnam's, 1980 [originally published 1935]), 48, 54. Herbert Croly, *The Promise of American Life* (New York: Dutton, 1963 [originally published 1909]), xix, 33, 35–36, 181–182. Dewey, "The Future of Liberalism" (1935), in Howard Zinn, *New Deal Thought* (Indianapolis: Bobbs-Merrill, 1966), 31 (the Founders' belief in eternal ideas is evil). Thomas G. West, "Progressivism and the Transformation of American Government," in *The Progressive Revolution in Politics and Political Science: Transforming the American Regime*, John Marini and Ken Masugi, eds. (Lanham: Rowman & Littlefield, 2005), 13–33 (how the modern liberal state departs in both theory and practice from the constitutionalism of the Founders). Ken I. Kersch, *Constructing Civil Liberties: Discontinuities in the Development of American Constitutional Law* (New York: Cambridge University Press, 2004), shows in convincing detail how twentieth-century Progressive liberalism deliberately undermined the Founders' conception of property, privacy, speech, and trial procedure rights for the sake of building the administrative state.

patrons. But this is precisely the character of government in the administrative state established by modern liberalism. Officials have an endless supply of honors, jobs, grants, set-asides, contracts, and outright handouts for their supporters, donors, and clients. From this point of view, "affirmative action," whatever its justice or injustice as policy, may be viewed as standard government practice in despotic governments. The rulers set up special privileges for whatever groups constitute their supporters and favorites.

This understanding of government is directly opposed to the Founders' view, as stated in the Massachusetts Declaration of Rights (1780):

> No man, nor corporation, or association of men, have any other title to obtain advantages, or particular and exclusive privileges, distinct from those of the community, than what arises from the consideration of services rendered to the public....; Government is instituted for the common good; for the protection, safety, prosperity and happiness of the people; and not for the profit, honor, or private interest of any one man, family, or class of men.[44]

The Founders hoped to build a political community where, in the words of the town of Boston's *Rights of the Colonists* (1772), there is "one rule of justice for rich and poor; for the favorite in court, and the country man at plow."[45] (The document was quoting John Locke's *Second Treatise*.)[46]

Some liberals openly favor rapid immigration precisely because it *is* undermining these older principles and traditions. As noted in the introduction to this volume, in 1991

---

44. Declaration of Rights, Articles 6 and 7, Massachusetts Constitution, 1780, in *The Founders' Constitution*, Kurland and Lerner, eds., 1:12.
45. Boston, Rights of the Colonists, 1772, in *Writings of Samuel Adams*, Harry A. Cushing, ed. (New York: Octagon Books, 1968 [originally published in 1904–1908]), 2:357.
46. Locke, *Second Treatise*, sec. 142.

Martha Riche, who soon afterwards became President Clinton's Director of the Census, said: "we have left the time when the nonwhite, non–Western part of our population could be expected to assimilate to the dominant majority. In the future, the white Western majority will have to do some assimilation of its own."[47]

Martha Riche's divisive view of America, in which the dominant way of life in America is treated as if it is based on race ("white"), stands at the opposite pole from the Founders' understanding of equality. The Founders thought that equality rightly understood requires government to secure the equal rights of every citizen, regardless of color or religion, on the basis of equal laws. The Founders wanted an immigration policy that brings people into the country at a pace and in a manner that would assimilate them into a way of life that is self–controlled, self–reliant, properly self–assertive, and based on the natural rights of all human beings, regardless of their race or ethnicity.

MODERN LIBERALISM AND CONSERVATISM AS OBSTACLES TO ASSIMILATION

Given the views and habits typical of immigrants today, those who share the perspective of the Founders will see an urgent need for them to be taught the principles and moral conduct of the American way of life, so that, as Washington wrote in the letter quoted earlier, "by an intermixture with our people, they, or their descendants, get assimilated to our customs, measures, and laws: in a word, soon become one people."[48] Perhaps the population of today's newcomers will become more like that of the natives as the years go

---

47. Riche is quoted in Brimelow, *Alien Nation*, 115.
48. Washington to the Vice President (John Adams), November 15, 1794, *Writings*, Fitzpatrick, ed., 34:23.

by, just as the descendants of the 1880–1914 immigration wave have voted, and acted more and more like the rest of America. But since the number of new arrivals is very large and is coming very rapidly, there is also a possible opposite effect, as Martha Riche anticipated: assimilation may go in the other direction, and Americans may become more like the immigrants. The U.S. Census Bureau reported that in 2005, 12.1 percent of the population (35 million people) was foreign born. Over one-fourth of that number (9 to 10 million, or 26 to 28 percent) consisted of illegal immigrants. The bulk of these illegals (69 percent in the 2000 census) were Mexicans. Some argue, convincingly, that the number of illegals is much higher than the Census Bureau number. The number could easily be well over 20 million.[49]

If earlier immigrants had difficulty assimilating to American beliefs and habits, when the country still had confidence that its way of life was the best in the world, how much more difficult will it be for today's newcomers to become Americans?

Some immigration advocates point out that today's foreign born numbers, as a proportion of the total population, are smaller than they were during the 1880–1914 period. In 1910, at the peak of the earlier immigration wave, 14.7

---

49. Steven A. Camarota, "Immigrants at Mid-Decade: A Snapshot of America's Foreign-Born Population in 2005," Center for Immigration Studies Backgrounder, December 2005, 1–2 (discussing foreign born and illegal immigrant population, based on U.S. Census Bureau, Current Population Survey: Annual Social and Economic Supplement, March 2005). A. Dianne Schmidley, *U.S. Census Bureau, Current Population Reports, Series P23-206, Profile of the Foreign-Born Population in the United States: 2000* (Washington: U.S. Government Printing Office, 2001), 9, 22, http://www.census.gov/prod/2002pubs/23-206.pdf (accessed July 8, 2005). There is convincing evidence that the Census Bureau underestimates the number of illegals: D. A. King, "Could There Be Twenty Million Illegals In the U.S.?" June 26, 2004, http://vdare.com/king/illegals.htm (accessed July 8, 2005).

percent of the population was foreign born, in contrast to 12.1 percent in 2005. But there is a massive difference between assimilation policies in that earlier period and today that renders the comparison doubtful. The percentage of immigrants who fail to assimilate is probably at its highest point in American history.

Before the 1960s, English was the language of American government, education, and business. Today government provides immigrants with interpreters when they seek public services, and it instructs their children in their native language in school. Businesses follow suit, with foreign-language or bilingual signs and forms becoming the norm in many parts of the country. This recalls the situation that led Benjamin Franklin in 1750s Pennsylvania to be alarmed for Americans' survival as *a people*: "Few of [the German immigrants'] children in the country learn English....[I]n our courts, the German business so increases that there is continual need of interpreters;...and I suppose in a few years they will also be necessary in the Assembly, to tell one half of our legislators what the other half say."[50] In Franklin's time, reduced levels of German immigration solved the problem. Around 1900, immigrants were quickly immersed in English in the public schools. Besides, the 1924 Immigration Act stopped the flow of immigrants for 40 years, allowing the process of assimilation to take hold. After 1965, when massive immigration once again became legal, and the laws against illegal immigration went largely unenforced, the failure of these newcomers to assimilate is now partly the result of intentional government policy. Exacerbating the situation, the effective result of the 1965 act was a tremendous increase of immigrants from Asia, Africa, and Latin America, and reduction to a trickle of immigration from Europe and European-stock nations.

---

50. Franklin, Letter to Collinson, May 9, 1753, *Writings*, 473.

On a deeper level, the unwillingness of government to insist on children learning English is only a symptom of a broad change in the attitudes of American leaders over the past half-century. America's elites have lost confidence that the American way of life—the way based on the founding principles—is good, against those who no longer believe that it is so. Consequently, America no longer teaches with its earlier assurance the habits and principles of liberty.

The American founding, and the political tradition based on the founding, are frequently denounced and mocked in textbooks and by leading scholars.[51] Consider property rights. The earlier view was that justice requires the protection of private property. Most Americans used to agree with these remarks of Abraham Lincoln:

> When one starts poor, as most do in the race of life, free society is such that he knows he can better his condition; he knows that there is no fixed condition of labor, for his whole life. I am not ashamed to confess that twenty-five years ago I was a hired laborer, nailing rails, at work on a flat-boat—just what might happen to any poor man's son. I want every man to have the chance—and I believe a black man is entitled to it—in which he *can* better his condition—when he can look forward and hope to be a hired laborer this year and next, work for himself afterward, and finally to hire men to work for him! That is the true system.[52]

In Lincoln's view, the typical American, like the typical immigrant, starts out poor, but he can get ahead in life by frugality, good sense, and hard work. In contrast, schools

---

51. West, *Vindicating the Founders*, xi–xii, 1–4, 17, 19, 71–75, 112, 148, 175.
52. Lincoln, Speech at New Haven, Conn., March 6, 1860, in *Collected Works of Abraham Lincoln*, Roy T. Basler, ed. (New Brunswick: Rutgers University Press, 1953), 4:24.

and textbooks today reject that position. Immigrants are no longer taught, as they were before the 1960s, to revere the Founders, Lincoln, and the principles of 1776. Instead, they are told that the most important fact about America's past is a shameful pattern of racism, sexism, and intolerance. It is no wonder, as Peter Skerry writes, that "contemporary political institutions and culture encourage Mexican–Americans to 'assimilate' precisely by defining themselves as an oppressed racial minority." This is what the dominant voices in society tell them, in school, at the movies, on television, and in the newspapers. It is no accident that many come to believe that they "cannot advance without the help of racially designated benefits."[53] What Skerry says of Mexican–Americans holds true, in varying degrees, of other immigrants as well.

Immigrants are told in effect that however irresponsibly they may live—whether they work or not, whether they have children in or out of wedlock—Americans will provide them and their children with food, health care, and housing. Government used to promote assimilation by means of free markets, minimal welfare, and the expectation of responsible moral conduct. Immigrant families and neighborhoods were encouraged to stand on their own through entrepreneurship, hard work, and moral restraint. We noted earlier that in recent years twice as many Mexican immigrant households as native households were using one or more of the major federal welfare programs, and that the percentage of babies born to unmarried Hispanics is almost twice that of non–Hispanic whites. Worse, as George Borjas has demonstrated, the rates of welfare dependency are actually going up for immigrant groups, the longer they stay in America. As for illegal immigrants, the first lesson they

---

53. Peter Skerry, *Mexican–Americans: The Ambivalent Minority* (New York: Free Press, 1993), 365, 8.

learn from the fact of their rarely contested entry is that the law is not taken seriously in America. It is so easy to enter the country illegally that about one million people did so in 1999, according to Steven Camarota. In sum, if assimilation is a problem today, government certainly shares the blame.[54]

Although, as I have indicated, questions may well be raised from the Founders' perspective concerning the liberal approach to assimilation, I cannot say that conservatives have an adequate response. For as I mentioned at the beginning of this essay, conservatives tend to be unaware that the principles of the founding require that citizens be formed not by qualities that are uniquely European or Christian or Biblical, but by qualities that reason can discover to be good and wholesome, independently of any religion or tradition. The reasonable principles of the founding are, as Lincoln said, an electric cord that can bind a nation of different religions and ethnicities together to make it a unified whole. But that will only be possible if the moral implications of those principles are understood and acted upon. Men must cultivate qualities of self–restraint, especially in their dealings with women and their offspring (in other words, they need to get married and try to stay married), and citizens

---

54. For the numbers on welfare and illegitimacy, see notes 29 and 32 above. George J. Borjas, *Friends or Strangers: The Impact of Immigrants on the U.S. Economy* (New York: Basic Books, 1990), 154–155 (growth of welfare dependency). See also Linda Chavez, *Out of the Barrio: Toward a New Politics of Hispanic Assimilation* (New York: Basic Books, 1991); Brimelow, *Alien Nation*, 216–221. Steven Camarota, "800,000 + Illegals Entering Annually in Late '90s," Press Release, Center for Immigration Studies, February 4, 2003, http://www.cis.org/articles /2003/illegalsrelease.html (accessed October 14, 2005). Reed Ueda, "Naturalization and Citizenship," in *Harvard Encyclopedia of American Ethnic Groups*, Stephan Thernstrom, ed. (Cambridge: Harvard University Press, 1980), 744–745. Oscar Handlin, *The Uprooted*, 2nd ed. (Boston: Little, Brown, 1973), 274–299.

must also develop sensible self–assertion and public–spirit-edness when it comes to defending their liberties.

IMMIGRATION AND THE FUTURE OF THE ADMINISTRATIVE STATE

The deepest challenge posed by immigration policy is whether America should or should not return to the proposition that all men are created equal, as that proposition was understood by the Founders. That is, the immigration question is inseparable from the question of the future of the administrative state, the future of modern liberalism. From the point of view of the American founding, not only immigration policy, but also family law, economic regulation, welfare, and many other policies will have to be reformed if the United States is to continue to "secure the blessings of liberty for ourselves and our posterity," including the posterity of immigrants.

As Jefferson foresaw, the longer the current immigration trend continues, the harder it will be to stop government's increasingly aggressive stance toward the traditional family; its policies that undermine the morality of self–restraint and of vigilant self–assertion; its growing limitations on the right to the free use of one's property; and its hostility toward political speech that it disapproves of. If the Founders' understanding was correct, then current immigration and citizenship policy threatens the American dream, which once promised, in Washington's words in his letter to the Hebrew Congregation at Newport, that "every one shall sit in safety under his own vine and fig tree, and there shall be none to make him afraid."[55]

What then is to be done? It is tempting to turn to pallia-tives, such as English–only ballots, deportation of criminal

---

55. Washington, *Writings*, Rhodehamel, ed., 767, quoting Micah 4:4.

aliens who have served their sentences, and building a fence along the Mexican border. In the current crisis, these would only be the first steps. With government actively discouraging assimilation to responsible citizenship, and with the scale of immigration, legal and illegal, being so vast, the best policy is more likely to be something much more comprehensive, such as an indefinite moratorium on almost all immigration combined with significant penalties for employers of illegal aliens as well as for the illegals themselves. Such a policy would encourage substantial numbers to return to their home countries. There could be exceptions for highly educated individuals who are fluent in English and who come from nations with long experience of the rule of law. But American liberty may prove to have a short future if the character of the body of citizens continues to be transformed as an easily predictable consequence of incorporating into the nation such massive numbers of those who do not understand and do not love the principles of responsible liberty.

Chapter 4

PROGRESSIVISM, IMMIGRATION AND CITIZENSHIP

John Marini

America has often been called a nation of immigrants as if that is what has distinguished it among the nations of the earth. But every human society that did not spring full blown from the soil with a common identity is a nation of strangers, or immigrants, who were somehow united in civic friendship. Some nations with long histories have forgotten their origins, or what it was that made it possible to distinguish themselves from others. The problem of immigration, therefore, is unintelligible in the absence of an understanding of what it is that constitutes the ground of unity or common identity. Any human association that considers itself as separate or distinct from other political societies—or, in modern times, one which considers itself sovereign—must make distinctions between those who are citizens and those who are not.

America established the ground of political citizenship in the equal natural rights of man. It required a social compact and consent to authorize the power of government. The social compact made it the primary purpose of government to protect the rights of individuals. By limiting the power of government, the compact assured the autonomy of civil society, making it unnecessary for religion to utilize the authority of government. Once equality is understood in terms of the equal protection of equal rights, considerations of religion, ethnicity, race, or culture cannot be decisive as the ground of citizenship, although they might have some prudential bearing on who might become citizens.

The philosophy of History and the new idea of the rational state which was at the core of the Progressive movement undermined the natural right foundation of the American regime. This resulted in the repudiation of the social contract and the principle of equality. The social compact and the natural right theory upon which it was based represented a philosophic way—through nature and reason—of understanding political and moral phenomenon. That tradition was fundamentally undermined by the acceptance of a philosophy of History. Joseph Cropsey characterized this transformation in human thought by observing that "the replacement of philosophy by history was the condition of the replacement of politics and religion by society and economics."[1]

In the rational state, the authority of science—and the new disciplines of the social sciences—would provide the theoretical and practical knowledge necessary to transform society and administer progress.[2] The Hegelian idea of the

---

1. Joseph Cropsey, "Karl Marx," in *History of Political Philosophy*, Leo Strauss and Joseph Cropsey, eds. (Chicago: Rand McNally, 1963), 722.

2. The scientific method would subsequently replace the faculty of reason as the means by which to make that knowledge useful to man. The social sciences, then, would become the applied science of the rational state. The crucial condition of the philosophy of History, or historicism, was the abandonment of the doctrine of natural right. The new sciences, therefore, rejected not only religion, but metaphysical reason—as well as prudence, or practical reason—in exchange for a scientific methodology. As Leo Strauss has observed, "historicism...stands or falls by the denial of the possibility of theoretical metaphysics and of philosophic ethics or natural right." *Natural Right and History* (Chicago: University of Chicago Press, 1953), 29.

state was meant to reestablish a political whole that would reunite the social and economic, the public and private, and make citizenship the ground of freedom and public virtue.[3] The Progressive thinkers, intoxicated by the new philosophy of History, looked to society and economics as fundamental to an understanding of the historical process. They gravitated, subsequently, to the concepts of *race* and *class,* and eventually, *culture,* as tangible factors in their attempts to elucidate that process. In their view, there are no permanent human problems. Consequently, every problem can be solved by the transformation of society and economics. That transformation required the rule of organized intelligence in the form of a rational bureaucracy within the state. The state itself becomes the embodiment of the whole and as such is an ethical organization. In denying the natural

---

3. Georg Wilhelm Hegel had established the philosophic ground of the world view which informed Progressivism. He did so in his comprehensive defense of the rational state, in which it would become possible to reconcile the particular and general will, or freedom and necessity. In Hegel's view, "the State is the mind on earth and consciously realizing itself there." It had replaced nature and nature's God. He observed that "the State is the divine Idea, as it exists on earth. In this perspective, the State is the precise object of world history in general. It is in the State that freedom attains its objectivity, and lives in the enjoyment of this objectivity. For the law of the State is the objectification of Spirit; it is will in its true form. Only the will that is obedient to the law is free. Insofar as the State, our country, constitutes a community of existence, and insofar as the subjective will of human beings submits to laws, the antithesis between freedom and necessity disappears. The rational is the necessary, the substantiality of a shared existence; and we are free to the extent that we acknowledge it as law, and follow it as the very substance of our being. The objective and subjective will are then reconciled, as one and the same serene whole." G.W. F. Hegel, *Introduction to the Philosophy of History*, Leo Rauch, trans. (Indianapolis: Hackett Publishers, 1988), 42. Accordingly, Hegel insisted that "man must therefore venerate the State as a secular deity." First and last quotes are from *Philosophy of Right*, T.M. Knox, trans. (London: Oxford University Press, 1942), 279, 285.

right foundation of philosophy, the truth of equality as the foundation of equal citizenship was also undermined.

The American Founders insisted that the abstract principle of natural equality spelled out the way in which all men are the same: in terms of their natural rights. But, the diversity in the faculties of men, and the factionalism which is derived from those differences, is also sown into the nature of man. This is recognition of the way in which men differ. Thus, social inequality, which grows out of the differences inherent in the faculties of men, is a necessary outcome of a free society. The defense of freedom, therefore, required a defense of property, understood in terms of the protection of the fundamental individual rights of conscience, opinion, interest, and labor. In separating church and state, government and civil society, and the public and private spheres, equality and liberty are reconciled in a reasonable way that is compatible with the nature of man.

Progressive thought, on the other hand, established a new ground of citizenship which rested on a denial of the doctrine of natural right and the older understanding of the principle of equality as an abstract truth. In addition, it denied the traditional view that freedom is subordinate to the moral law. It is the new historical understanding of freedom and equality which would provide the foundation of equal citizenship in Progressivism. In the modern state, rationalization, or centralization, then, would require the imposition of a governmental uniformity upon civil society, without regard to individual rights or natural differences.

The philosophy of History, therefore, established a new ground by which to determine the common good. That new understanding provided the foundation upon which citizenship would depend—the creation of a rational, or organic, will. By the end of the nineteenth century, the two tangible forces most descriptive of economy and society, *class* and *race*, had gained the ascendancy over every other category of knowledge providing the ideological foundation for the understanding and exercise of will. Both forces would be discredited in the twentieth century, but long before race theory was discredited politically by Hitler and the Nazis, it had gained intellectual respectability in the natural and social sciences. Indeed, race theory had become so pervasive during the first part of the twentieth century that Hannah Arendt, writing during World War II, noted:

> Among ideologies few have won enough prominence to survive the hard competitive struggle of persuasion, and only two have come out on top and essentially defeated all others; the ideology which interprets history as an economic struggle of classes, and the other that interprets history as a natural fight of races. The appeal of both to large masses was so strong that they were able to obtain state support and establish themselves as official national doctrines. But far beyond the boundaries in which race–thinking and class–thinking have developed into obligatory patterns of thought, free public opinion has adopted them to such an extent that not only intellectuals but great masses of people will no longer accept any presentation of past or present facts that is not in agreement with these views.[4]

Although the notion of racial superiority was repudiated in the aftermath of the Second World War, the understanding of history, which made racial theory credible, retained its authority. Perhaps in the twenty–first century it still holds sway. As Arendt surmised before the middle of the last century, any objective understanding of the historical past or present outside of the categories of race and class has had little resonance among intellectuals or the mass public. There is little doubt that class, understood in an

---

4. Hannah Arendt, "Race–Thinking Before Racism," *The Review of Politics*, January 1944, vol. 6, no. 1, 38–39.

historicist manner, however discredited by the political demise of Communism, is still the most useful way in which to evaluate economics and politics in the disciplines of the social sciences. Race has been thoroughly discredited in politics and theory. It has, however, attained a new status as a moral phenomenon, primarily as a symbol of exploitation that would become the ground of group solidarity.

In its origins, race was an important element in the philosophic understanding of history; but it was not the decisive element. While the very real historical events of the twentieth century discredited the political theory of racial superiority, the difficulty of separating the category of race from History has remained. Even when the natural and social sciences began to doubt the authority of race as an explanation for legitimizing political power, it remained a fundamental category in the understanding of identity and citizenship. In his attempt to make sense of that term at the beginning of the twentieth century, Henry Adams noted in *The Education of Henry Adams:* "History offered a feeble and delusive smile at the sound of the word *race;* evolutionists and ethnologists disputed its very existence; no one knew what to make of it; yet, without the clue, history was a fairy tale."[5]

The great tragedies spawned by the Nazi and Communist parties, although defeated as political movements, did not result in a rejection of the ideological ground that engendered them. By the end of the twentieth century, it was clear that mass and elite opinion had not gone beyond the categories of race and class. Despite the fact that political rhetoric in America had proclaimed equality as the fundamental goal, the theoretical ground of the principle of equality had been undermined by the philosophy of

5. Henry Adams, *The Education of Henry Adams* (New York: Modern Library, 1931), 411–412.

History. It has never been restored. Consequently, the leading intellectual movements of our time provide seemingly endless variations on the historical categories of race and class. The postmodern movements, political, social, or cultural, which have looked to establish identity in the categories of race, sexual orientation, or gender, are themselves offshoots of the evolution of historical consciousness.

Despite the Civil Rights movements of the last half–century, ostensibly based on the principle of equality, nearly every political and administrative solution to the problem of equal rights has required an unequal treatment of individual citizens. In practice, therefore, the public policies of the administrative state have not been based upon any understanding of the social compact. The principle of equality, understood in terms of the natural rights of individuals, could no longer serve as the foundation of citizenship. Rather, the new notion of citizenship presupposed the necessity of subordinating individual rights to the fundamental requirements of the administrative state. Consequently, the notion of citizenship as a tangible or meaningful thing has resonance only within the framework of the historical categories of race, class, or culture. It is not surprising, therefore, that within the policymaking apparatus of the administrative state group rights provide the best—perhaps the only—way to establish identity as a member of the state.

As a result, it has become nearly impossible in the administrative state to execute public policies in any way other than the unequal treatment of individual citizens. This undermining of the principle of equality, and the regime of civil and religious liberty, after the Civil War transformed the meaning of citizenship. It was inevitable that this transformed meaning would have a profound effect upon the problem of immigration. Consequently, it was not merely the influx of aliens that could change a nation; ideas have transformed the meaning of citizenship for the native born as well. Moreover, immigrants, too, are shaped by the regime which accepts them. They typically adapt to whatever they perceive as the expectations and aspirations of that regime. Not surprisingly, the expectations and aspirations of citizenship in a regime of civil and religious liberty (for natives and immigrants alike) are far different than those expectations which have been created within the administrative, or welfare, state. It is necessary, therefore, to elucidate the relationship between the idea of regime and the notion of citizenship as it developed in America.

The American Founders established a foundation of citizenship unlike any that the world had ever seen. It was not based on religion, nationality, race, or any previous category of citizenship. It was based on the acceptance of an idea, the natural equality of all men. Although nearly all immigrants would come from countries shaped by those previous categories of citizenship, none of them could be fundamental as the foundation of American citizenship. Therefore, immigration policy would have to be decided on a prudential basis, which would allow exclusion on numerous practical grounds. The understanding of equality as the foundation of citizenship is necessary but not sufficient in itself. It is also essential to take into account the problem of the character of prospective citizens, or their capacity for self–government. This, too, poses a practical problem in a regime in which there is no historical antecedent.

It is not altogether apparent what kind of regime—or, categories of citizenship, religion, nationality, color—has established the proper kind of character for inclusion in a regime in which equality and liberty constitute the basis of citizenship. At the time of the American founding, religious belief was thought to be fundamental in determining the capacity for citizenship. It was necessary, therefore, to understand equality as a principle in order to see that it was possible, within a social compact, to have different religious beliefs and yet be fellow citizens. What are the differences among human beings that can be reconciled within the social compact, and what are those that cannot be reconciled? An understanding of human nature is helpful, but most differences of citizenship—like those of the regimes that produced them—are conventional.

However, no matter what the answer to the question of the differences of character, the American regime had to establish whatever prudential considerations that were thought necessary in terms of restricting immigration to those who could best be assimilated into the social compact. Still, no older category of citizenship, even though it might have established the character of decent citizens in previous regimes, could serve as the exclusive ground of citizenship, especially if it undermined the principles of the social compact. Yet, in the period after the Civil War, that is precisely what happened. Progressive intellectuals, animated by a new understanding of history that resulted in a rejection of natural right, denied that the idea of equality could establish the foundation of citizenship in the modern state. Armed with the authority of science, they came to believe that capacity for citizenship was dependent upon race, class, or subsequently, culture.

The twentieth century has made it clear that the problems of immigration and citizenship have become almost impossible to understand on prudential or practical grounds. Thus any considerations of means, or moral capacity, the things necessary for understanding character, are no longer thought to be relevant to the discussion of citizenship. The category of race, established as the ground of morality in the state because it is the embodiment of the will of a people, had become an end in itself. Thus the notion of race had replaced the principle of equality as the ground of the meaning of citizenship. As a result, every prudential argument is quickly condemned as racist by the intellectuals and increasingly the politicians and public as well. It has not been easy to reestablish the idea of equality as the foundation of the regime. Consequently, even those principled pieces of legislation, such as the Civil Rights Act of 1964, have not been interpreted on the basis of an understanding of the principle of equality but in terms of the historical categories of race or class. It is important, therefore, to understand the meaning of citizenship in a regime of civil and religious liberty before it becomes possible to see how and why it differs from the notion of citizenship in the administrative state.

CITIZENSHIP IN A REGIME OF CIVIL AND RELIGIOUS LIBERTY

American statesmen from Washington to Lincoln understood America as a regime of civil and religious liberty.[6]

---

6. Thomas Paine, himself an immigrant, called America "the asylum for the persecuted lovers of civil and religious liberty from every part of Europe." George Washington, in a letter to Lucretia Van Winter, noted: "At best I have only been an instrument in the hands of Providence, to effect a revolution which is interesting to the general liberties of mankind, and to the emancipation of a country which may afford an Asylum, if we are wise enough to pursue the paths wch. lead to virtue and happiness, to the oppressed and needy of the Earth. Our region is extensive, our plains productive, and if they are cultivated with liberality and good sense, we may be happy ourselves, and diffuse happiness to all who wish to participate." The Paine and Washington quotes are in *Immigration and the American Tradition*, Moses Rischin, ed. (Indianapolis: Bobbs–Merrill, 1976), 34, 43–44. George Washington noted his reason for fighting the British: "the establishment of Civil and Religious Liberty was the motive which induced me to the field." Quoted in Charles Kesler, "The Promise of American Citizenship," in *Immigration and Citizenship in the Twenty-First Century*, Noah M. J. Pickus, ed. (Lanham: Rowman & Littlefield, 1998), 12.

The uniqueness of America, they thought, was to be seen in the manner in which it was able to reconcile politics and religion, civil and religious liberty, or, freedom and morality.[7] They understood man and citizenship—and man's capacity for self–rule and the desire for freedom—in the light of human nature.

In most European nations a common morality and religion, or faith, was the ground of citizenship. However, after the Protestant Reformation religion itself was a source of division among Christians.[8] Religion could no longer serve as the authority for political life and citizenship. A common religion, in which *individuals* shared a common faith, had established a means for determining the moral basis of self–government. But religious differences among the various Protestant and Catholic sects had only provided the occasion for bloody warfare.

---

7. Alexis de Tocqueville, too, had grasped the importance of the ability of Americans to reconcile "the spirit of religion and the spirit of liberty." He pointed to the reason why it had become possible to reconcile religion and politics, and morality and liberty. He observed that "religion perceives that civil liberty affords a noble exercise to the faculties of man and that the political world is a field prepared by the Creator for the efforts of mind. Free and powerful in its own sphere, satisfied with the place reserved for it, religion never more surely establishes its empire than when it reigns in the hearts of men unsupported by aught beside its native strength. Liberty regards religion as its companion in all its battles and its triumphs, as the cradle of its infancy and the divine source of its claims. It considers religion as the safeguard of morality, and morality as the best security of law and the surest pledge of the duration of freedom." *Democracy in America* (New York: Vintage Books, 1945), 2:45.
8. Religion, consequently, always played an important role in civil society, even after it had ceased to establish the ground of citizenship. As John Higham has noted, "By far the oldest and—in early America—the most powerful of the anti–foreign traditions came out of the shock of the Reformation. Protestant hatred of Rome played so large a part in pre–Civil War nativist thinking that historians have sometimes regarded nativism and anti–Catholicism as more or less synonymous." John Higham, *Strangers in the Land* (New Brunswick: Rutgers University Press, 1955), 5.

Although the religious doctrines of certain Christian sects appeared to be compatible with freedom and self–government, others seemed to foster a dependency which perpetuated despotic rule. The European nations shared a common religion, but Christianity itself had not established the conditions for a common citizenship. "For when pressed into political service," Charles Kesler has observed,

> Christianity—a religion centered around belief in Christ rather than obedience to a revealed code of laws (e.g. Torah or *shari'a*)—had the distressing if somewhat paradoxical tendency both to deflate civil laws' significance and to inflate their pretensions. That is, the pursuit of true Christianity tempted some believers to desert the earthly for the heavenly city, but tempted others to commandeer temporal laws in order to enforce the faith. The one tendency sapped the foundations of citizenship; the other turned citizenship into fanaticism.[9]

The solution to the problem of citizenship, therefore, required a solution to the problem of religion. Kesler suggests that

> [b]y building government on the basis of natural rights and the social contract, the American Founders showed how, for the first time since the days of the Holy Roman Empire, men could be good citizens of the City of God and good citizens of their earthly city without injury or insult to either...[T]he key to the solution was the insistence that questions of revealed truth be excluded from determination by the political sovereign or by political majorities. Indeed, majority rule and minority rights could be made consistent only on this basis. Under modern conditions, limited government thus becomes essential to the rule of law.[10]

---

9. Charles R. Kesler, "The Promise of American Citizenship," in *Immigration and Citizenship*, 14.
10. Ibid.

The structure of republican government and its democratic processes are made possible only upon recognition of the fact that moral authority does not emanate from government or from majorities. It was the new understanding of natural right, and the political doctrine of equality, that had established a foundation for individual rights. The social compact, therefore, provided the theoretical and moral basis for majority rule. At the same time, it was necessary to limit the power of a numerical majority to the protection of the rights of each on behalf of the rights of all. It was for this reason that it was possible for George Washington to celebrate the fact that America had extended the rights of citizenship to Jews, probably for the first time in the modern history of a Western nation. In his letter to the Hebrew congregation in Newport, in 1790, Washington stated the reason why this was so:

> The citizens of the United States of America have the right to applaud themselves for having given to mankind examples of an enlarged and liberal policy worthy of imitation. All possess alike liberty of conscience and immunities of citizenship. It is now no more that toleration is spoken of as if it were by the indulgence of one class of citizens that another enjoyed the exercise of their inherent natural rights, for happily the Government of the United States, which gives to bigotry no sanction, to persecution no assistance, requires only that they who live under its protection should demean themselves as good citizens in giving it on all occasions their effectual support.[11]

The great achievement of the American Founders was to establish a solution to the problem of political obligation which had eluded Western man since the collapse of the Roman Empire. As Kesler has observed:

---

11. Quoted in Thomas G. West, *Vindicating the Founders* (Lanham: Rowman & Littlefield, 1997), 149.

> Civil liberty meant finding a new ground for law and citizenship that would protect decent politics from arbitrary claims of divine right. Religious liberty meant separating church membership from citizenship in order to protect the conscientious pursuit of true religion from civil or ecclesiastical tyranny. Civil liberty and religious liberty have the same root, a theoretical or philosophical insight: the doctrine of natural rights.[12]

In practice, that philosophic doctrine required the separation of church and state, which made it necessary to separate politics or government from civil society, thereby distinguishing the public and private spheres. It was this doctrine that established the ground of modern constitutionalism. The view of America as a regime of civil and religious liberty lasted only so long as the tradition of natural right remained viable.

The American founding, through toleration of religion, showed that it was no longer necessary to share a common faith as a fundamental requirement of citizenship. Furthermore, the ground of citizenship would no longer rest upon color or a common blood. The acceptance of the principles of the American founding made it necessary to establish the foundation of equal citizenship on the natural rights of man. As Abraham Lincoln noted prior to the Civil War, immigrants who had come to America, although unrelated to the Founders by blood, found that they had something in common that was more important than ties of blood. Lincoln observed that

> if they look back through this history to trace their connection with those days by blood, they have none, but when they look through that old Declaration of Independence they find that those old men say that "We hold

---

12. Kesler, "The Promise of American Citizenship," in *Immigration and Citizenship*, 33–34.

these truths to be self–evident, that all men are created equal," and then they feel that that moral sentiment
taught in that day evidences their relation to those men,
that it is the father of all moral principle in them, and that
they have a right to claim it as though they were blood of
the blood, and flesh of the flesh, of the men who wrote
that Declaration—and so they are.[13]

What was to become indispensable as the ground of citizenship, therefore, was recognition of an abstract truth—that
all men are created equal.

The new understanding of citizenship, which had important ramifications for the problem of immigration, required
an almost philosophic defense of the principle of equality.
Furthermore, knowledge of the meaning of equality is only
the necessary, but not the sufficient, condition for establishing the social compact. It is also important that prospective
citizens have the capacity for self–government, or the right
kind of character—one compatible with the exercise of freedom and its defense—in order to perpetuate the regime. But
in such a regime, there is no tangible factor, in terms of religion, race, or nationality, by which to determine the basis
of citizenship. Practically speaking, therefore, immigration
into America would of necessity be understood in a prudential manner. But the question arises: what determines
the proper kind of character for a regime in which equality
and liberty constitute the foundation of the compact. Religion, nationality, race, or the kind of regime—despotic or
not—are all things that will be taken into consideration.

Interestingly, the Immigration Act of 1790 is often cited
as support for the view that the American Founders understood immigration and citizenship in terms of race. That
act was an attempt to facilitate the quick naturalization of
immigrants—in only two years. European whites, of course,

---

13. Quoted in West, 147.

would be those best equipped to become citizens so quickly. The act, then, was based on excluding those—particularly Indians and blacks who were, or had been, slaves. It was not color or race, but civilization, which was the standard for their judgment. The former slaves and savages were not sufficiently civilized to have developed the kind of education, manners, and especially the deliberative capacity necessary to participate in the social compact. The problem of immigration, therefore, was understood in a prudential way that was compatible with an understanding of nature and reason. The idea that race—as a biological category, understood through history and science—could be more fundamental in terms of understanding man's humanity than reflection upon human nature or reason, was not intelligible to the Founders. It was not until the end of the nineteenth century that such an historicist understanding of man would become legitimized in the science of biology. The Founders did not understand man, or race, in terms of history, science, or biology. Rather, they understood man in terms of nature and the cultivation of reason—or lack thereof.

The American Founders were not oblivious to the fact that there would be immigrants from particular regimes who could not be easily assimilated. As a result, prudence would require the necessity of extending residency requirements for such immigrants. When the Federalists passed the Alien and Sedition Act, they extended the number of years necessary for naturalization to fourteen (as opposed to two in the old act). They were concerned that the increase of immigrants from Europe, many of whom had fled the French Revolution and were thought to have the kind of habits of character that could be modified by association with free citizens, would require a longer period of naturalization. Of course, those prudential arguments could not be separated from the political problems of the time, and therefore they can be sound or unsound in terms of policy. However, no policy based on prudence, which is concerned with means, should have the effect of undermining the end or principle of the regime.

Citizenship in a free society could encompass many differences based on religious, ethnic, or racial, grounds. It would be necessary, of course, that those who established the compact consent to the fact that all of those differences can be accommodated on the ground of equality. But immigration policy could not be indifferent to the moral character of its prospective citizens. Therefore prudence would dictate that those immigrants would be best suited who were most capable of grasping and appreciating the principles of equality and liberty. It would be those who were self-reliant and most interested in self-government who would be encouraged to become citizens. Most importantly, there could be no expectation that government should extend privileges to any group, or deny the rights of any individual. Immigration could in no way undermine the principles of the social compact which provided the foundations of citizenship for those who had established it.

In 1819, John Quincy Adams illustrated the importance of this fundamental necessity. He gave the following reply to a German immigrant who wondered why America had not adopted measures to encourage immigrants from Europe by extending favors on their behalf. Adams noted that Americans were not "in any manner insensible to the great benefits" of immigration,

> but there is one principle which pervades all the institutions of this country, and which must always operate as an obstacle to the granting of favors to new comers. This is a land, not of *privileges*, but of *equal rights*. Privileges are granted by European sovereigns to particular classes of individuals, for purposes of general policy; but the general impression here is that *privileges* granted to one

> denomination of people, can very seldom be discriminated
> from erosions of the rights of others. But hence it is that
> no government in the world possesses so few means of
> bestowing favors, as the government of the United States.
> If the powers, however, of the government to do good are
> restricted, those of doing harm are still more limited.[14]

Immigration policies, understood in light of the social compact, could offer no more than freedom and opportunity to
prospective citizens. A government or society which offered
incentives and privileges to newcomers could do so only at
the expense of the equal rights of all citizens.

The American Founders established a new ground of
citizenship compatible with an understanding that equality
and freedom was subordinate to the moral law. That view
required the protection of the freedom of the mind and conscience, which meant the free exercise of religion. Thus the
Founders for the first time solved the problem of political
obligation in a democratic manner. This had become possible because of the rediscovery of the doctrine of natural
right. The social compact, based on the principle of equality, would give rise to a free society. A free society would in
turn require the necessity of distinguishing the sacred and
secular, the political and social, and the public and private
spheres.

The new Progressive political thought, on the other
hand, denied natural right and the social compact. Through
the idea of the state, Progressivism hoped to establish a new
conception of government and citizenship, one that would
empower government to reorder the economy and society
with the purpose of resolving the tension between the individual and society, or between freedom and necessity. With
the establishment of the modern administrative state, the

---

14. John Quincy Adams, quoted in *Immigration and the American Tradition*, Moses Rischin, ed. (Indianapolis: Bobbs–Merrill , 1976), 46.

role of government could not be understood to be the protection of the individual natural rights of citizens. Consequently, the social compact would become meaningless.

HISTORY, SCIENCE AND RACE

The ideas of natural right and the social compact had animated the early American understanding of citizenship and immigration. With the acceptance of historicist—or Progressive—thought in the period after the Civil War, the foundation and meaning of citizenship was fundamentally altered. That transformation had a profound effect on the problem of immigration as well. The political meaning of equality had rested upon an understanding of man as a rational and moral being. As long as nature provided the standard by which to judge political right, freedom and equality were understood to be subordinate to the moral law. In the modern state, a new understanding of freedom would become the foundation of morality and citizenship.

Rousseau's denial of the view that rationality constituted the distinction between man and the animals led him to conclude that man has no nature, only a capacity for self–perfection.[15] He argued: "therefore it is not so much under-

---

15. It is in the notion of self–perfection, or perfectibility, that the prospect of a glorious future finds its justification. Charles Beard provides an example of the extravagant hope placed upon a new understanding of the future and its vehicle, the rational State. Beard insisted that "the highest type of modern citizen [is one] who surrenders the hope of private gain that he may serve the state. The eighteenth–century philosophers were wrong. We have not been driven from a political paradise; we have not fallen from a high estate, nor is there any final mold into which society can be cast. On the contrary, society has come from crude and formless associations beginning in a dim and dateless past and moves outward into an illimitable future, which many of us believe will not be hideous and mean, but beautiful and magnificent. In this dynamic society, the citizen becomes the co–worker in that great and indivisible process which

standing which constitutes the distinction of man among the animals as it is his being a free agent...It is above all in the consciousness of this freedom that the spirituality of his soul is shown."[16] After Rousseau, freedom would no longer be understood in terms of the nature of man, nor could it be subordinate to the moral law. Rather, freedom, or will, would become the foundation of morality. The political problem was then one of creating a general, or moral, will.

It is difficult to overstate the importance of consciousness of freedom and the idea of perfectibility in the minds of the Progressive intellectuals. Thus Herbert Croly, one of the most important Progressive intellectuals of the early twentieth century, insisted that "democracy must stand or fall on a platform of possible human perfectibility."[17] Croly measured the progress of man in terms of his willingness to serve his fellow man. "If it be true that democracy is based upon the assumption that every man shall serve his fellow-man, the organization of democracy should be gradually adapted to that assumption."[18] Nonetheless, Croly was well aware that

> [t]he majority of men cannot be made disinterested for life by exhortation, by religious services, by any expenditure of subsidized works, or even by grave and manifest

---

draws down granite hills and upbuilds great nations." Charles Beard, "Politics," in *Discipline and History: Political Science in the United States,* James Farr and Raymond Seidelman, eds. (Ann Arbor: University of Michigan Press, 1993), 118. Woodrow Wilson, too, believed that the idea of progress was a modern discovery. Unlike previous generations, Wilson noted, "we think of the future, not the past, as the more glorious time in comparison with which the present is nothing." "What is Progress," in *The New Freedom,* (New York: Doubleday, Page & Co., 1913), 39.

16. Jean Jacques Rousseau, *Second Discourse,* Roger Masters, trans. (New York: St. Martin's Press, 1964), 114.

17. Herbert Croly, *The Promise of American Life* (Cambridge: Harvard University Press, 1965), 418.

18. Ibid.

> public need. They can be made permanently unselfish
> only by being helped to become disinterested in their
> individual purposes. In the complete democracy a man
> must in some way be made to serve the nation in the
> very act of contributing to his own individual fulfillment.
> Not until his personal action is dictated by disinterested
> motives can there be any such harmony between private
> and public interests.[19]

The bureaucracy, by creating the occupations to be established within the administrative state, would become the means of reconciling private and public interests, or the particular and general will.

It was the German theorists, primarily Kant and Hegel, who established the ground of humanity—and subsequently citizenship in the state—upon the new understanding of freedom and the cultivation of moral will. Because man was now understood to have made himself human through his own efforts, or in the course of his history, it was no longer possible to understand nature and reason as the fundamental attributes of man's humanity. Rather, it is the capacity for, and consciousness of, freedom which distinguished man among the animals. The process by which man had made himself human through the use of his freedom, or will, was a result of his ability to adapt and transform his environment in the course of history.

Subsequently, the tangible ingredients by which to identify the evolution of social and economic man would come to be understood through the concepts of race, class, or variations of those categories—concrete factors such as geography, climate, and language. These things taken together with art and civil religion would, after the influence of Hegel, come to be understood as culture. In looking at the historical differences in the progress of the evolution

---

19. Ibid.

of man, it was not long before it was thought possible to measure the superiority of different peoples and classes or groups. In undermining the natural right foundation of individual citizenship, moral will, based on the new understanding of freedom, was legitimized within the concept of the state.

One important American Progressive, Mary Parker Follett, in *The New State*, written early in the twentieth century, outlined the new Progressive understanding of freedom and rights. She noted:

> Democracy has meant to many "natural" rights, "liberty" and "equality." The acceptance of the group principle defines for us in truer fashion those watchwords of the past. If my true self is the group–self, then my only rights are those which membership in a group gives me. The old idea of natural rights postulated the particularist individual; we know now that no such person exists. The group and the individual come into existence simultaneously: with this group–man appear group–rights. Thus man can have no rights apart from society or independent of society or against society. Particularist rights are ruled out as everything particularist is ruled out...The truth of the whole matter is that our only concern with "rights" is not to protect them but to create them. Our efforts are to be bent not upon guarding the rights which Heaven has showered upon us, but in creating all the rights we shall ever have.[20]

In Follett's view, those rights had to be understood in terms of the group and not the individual. Thus she noted:

> As an understanding of the group process abolishes "individual rights," so it gives us a true definition of liberty.

---

20. Mary Parker Follett, *The New State, Group Organization the Solution of Popular Government* (New York: Longmans, Green and Co., 1923 [originally published in 1918]), 138.

We have seen that the free man is he who actualizes the will of the whole. I have no liberty except as an essential member of a group...But liberty is not measured by the number of restraints we do not have, but by the number of spontaneous activities we do have... We see that to obey the group which we have helped to make and of which we are an integral part is to be free because we are then obeying ourselves. Ideally the state is such a group, actually it is not, but it depends upon us to make it more and more so. The state must be no external authority which restrains and regulates me, but it must be myself acting as the state in every smallest detail of life. Expression, not restraint, is always the motive of the ideal state.[21]

The Progressive understanding of freedom and citizenship necessitated the rejection of the notion of individual private rights because individuals would become free as citizens only when they exercised their will on behalf of the group, or ultimately participated as members of the ethical state, understood as the embodiment of the organic will of a people. John Dewey had expressed much this same view a generation before Mary Parker Follett. In an early essay, the *Ethics of Democracy*, published in 1888, Dewey observed that

[t]he essence of the "Social Compact" theory is not the idea of the formulation of a contract; it is the idea that men are mere individuals, without any social relations *until* they form a contract...Society, as a real whole, is the normal order, and the mass as an aggregate of isolated units is the fiction. If this be the case, and if democracy be a form of society, it not only does have, but must have, a common will; for it is this unity of will which makes it an organism. A state represents men so far as they have become organically related to one another, or are possessed of unity of purpose and interest...But human society represents a more perfect organism. The whole lives truly in

---

21. Ibid., 138.

every member, and there is no longer the appearance of aggregation, or continuity. The organism manifests itself as what it truly is, an ideal or spiritual life, a unity of *will*. If, then, society and the individual are really organic to each other, then the individual is society concentrated...In conception, at least, democracy approaches most nearly the ideal of all social organization; that in which the individual and society are organic to each other...The organism must have its spiritual organs; having a common will it must express it.[22]

Mary Parker Follett had contended that "as the collective idea and the collective will, right and purpose, are born within the all–sufficing social process, so here too the individual finds the wellspring of his life."[23] The individual will and collective purpose is reconciled within the social process of the group, which taken as a whole becomes the moral will within the modern state. Therefore, the group process and social—or organized—intelligence becomes institutionalized in the regulatory apparatus of the administrative state. Thus, the state, because it encompasses an organic social and ethical whole, produces within itself the technical or rational means—the bureaucracy—which can enable it to establish policies for carrying out the will of the people. With the establishment of the scientific method, Charles Merriam, a celebrated political theorist of the time, observed that "[p]olitics as the art of the traditional advances to politics as the science of constructive social control."[24] Thus, the modern state would require centralized control of the political, social and economic spheres. Subsequently, the Progressives would argue that the unity

---

22. John Dewey, *Ethics of Democracy* (Ann Arbor: Andrews and Company, 1888), 6, 7, 13–15.
23. Follett, 60.
24. Quoted in John G. Gunnell, *The Descent of Political Theory* (Chicago: University of Chicago Press, 1993), 99.

of the citizenry would necessitate a commonality of race or common blood.[25]

EQUALITY AND CITIZENSHIP

Modern science and the philosophy of History had not only transformed the meaning of freedom, but the understanding of equality and citizenship as well. The categories of race and class had become central to the elucidation of man as an historical being. Interestingly, the most important battleground in the Progressives' attempts to undermine the natural right foundation of the social compact came to revolve around the interpretation of the meaning of the American Civil War. The Progressives hoped to replace the old view of the social compact with the new Hegelian understanding of the modern state. During the Civil War, Lincoln had defended America as a regime of civil and religious liberty. In his view, the social compact had established the political conditions of equality and liberty. Slavery was incompatible with both equality and liberty when understood in light of nature and philosophic reason.

The Civil War, as Abraham Lincoln always insisted, was about the issue of slavery and was fought over the principle of equality. With the victory of the Union armies, it seemed likely that Lincoln's understanding of the meaning of equality would prevail. In that case, equality would have remained the indispensable ground of national citizenship. But such was not to be the case. The Progressive intellectuals, and the new social science disciplines then being developed in the new research universities, denied the natural right foundation of the regime. They also rejected the social compact

---

25. See Daniel Tichenor, *Dividing Lines: The Politics of Immigration Control in America* (Princeton: Princeton University Press, 2002), 75–97.

and the abstract principle of equality itself. Charles Merriam explained the reason for the rejection. He noted: "the influence of the German school is most obvious in relation to the contract theory of the origin of the state and the idea of the function of the state. The theory that the state originates in an agreement between men was assailed by the German thinkers and the historical, organic, evolutionary idea substituted for it." Merriam was well aware that:

> Considering the question as one of principle, it is evident that much depends on one's political theory. If we believe that government has no jurisdiction over men unless they have consented to it, and that every man is entitled to equal civil and political rights, regardless of his fitness for them, then it follows that to deprive any man of the suffrage for any cause, or any people of self-government for any cause, is a departure from democratic principles... If on the other hand, it is believed that liberty and rights are necessarily conditioned upon political capacity, and that the consent of the governed is a principle which, in the present state of affairs, cannot be perfectly realized, then the situation is altered.[26]

Nor was Merriam alone in his defense of Southern principles. Herbert Croly, the great Progressive reformer, agreed with Merriam and the slave owners. The slave holders were correct in their view, Croly insisted, because "negroes were a race possessed of moral and intellectual qualities inferior to those of white men."[27] In the view of the Progressive intellectuals, man is a historical being, and history, not nature, had determined what it means to be a human being. The struggle among the races in history determined the race

26. Charles Edward Merriam, *A History of American Political Theories* (New York: The Macmillan Company, 1910), 346.
27. Herbert Croly, *The Promise of American Life* (Cambridge: Harvard University Press, 1965), 81.

that deserved to be on top. The superiority of the white race and the inferiority of the black race is the scientific proof of the inequality of men. This proof had become evident as a result of the evolutionary theory of human development. Furthermore, they insisted that, if individual rights cannot be derived from the principle of equality, the source of legitimacy, or right, is derived from the state and its laws, not nature.

Abraham Lincoln was admired, and even revered, by many of the Progressive intellectuals. But, it was not because he had anchored the moral authority of the regime in the principle of equality. That view would have made it impossible to defend political inequality on any ground whatsoever. Moreover, the Progressives denied what Lincoln affirmed, that the foundation of the social compact rested upon an understanding of natural right. The Progressive intellectual and political movements, whether animated by Social Darwinism, socialism, anarchism, or communism, were united in rejecting the natural rights foundation of the social compact. Rather, they came to embrace the modern idea of the state. Charles Merriam was typical of the Progressive intellectuals. He noted: "the present tendency is to disregard the once dominant ideas of natural rights and the social contract...The origin of the state is regarded, not as the result of a deliberate agreement among men, but as the result of historical development, instinctive rather than conscious; and rights are considered to have their source not in nature, but in law."[28]

Merriam was not unique in his view that the American Founders had misunderstood the meaning of liberty. He was well aware that the Southern opinion had differed from the view of the Founders. Furthermore, in looking at recent

---

28. Charles Edward Merriam, *A History of American Political Theories*, 311.

trends in scholarship, Merriam observed:

> The modern school has, indeed, formulated a new idea of liberty, widely different from that taught in the early years of the Republic. The "Fathers" believed that in the original state of nature all men enjoy perfect liberty, that they surrender a part of this liberty in order that the government may be organized, and that therefore the stronger the government, the less the liberty remaining to the individual. Liberty is, in short, the natural and inherent right of all men; government the necessary limitation of this liberty. Calhoun and his school, as it has been shown, repudiated this idea, and maintained that liberty is not the natural right of all men, but only the reward of the races or individuals properly qualified for its possession. Upon this basis, slavery was defended against the charge that it was inconsistent with human freedom, and in this sense and so applied; the theory was not accepted outside the South. The mistaken application of the idea had the effect of delaying recognition of the truth in what had been said until the controversy over slavery was at an end."[29]

The remarkable assertion that slavery had obscured the truth of the historical and scientific fact that race established the ground of liberty and political right was not uncommon among the Progressives. Merriam, consequently, agreed with Calhoun that "not only are men created unequal...but this very inequality must be regarded as one of the essential conditions of human progress...This fundamental fact that individuals or races are unequal is not an argument against, but rather in favor of, social and political advancement."[30]

It is not surprising, therefore, that the new disciplines of the social sciences, including political science, were almost unanimous in their rejection of the doctrine of natural right,

29. Ibid., 311–312.
30. Ibid., 230.

the principle of equality and the social compact. The social sciences rejected slavery, but the rejection was on the ground that slavery was an historical anachronism. This view was confirmed by the events of history, as evidenced in the victory of the Union armies. It made it possible, subsequently, to defend the new scientific understanding that political capacity, or the suitability for self–government and freedom, was dependent upon the progress of the races. As Merriam had noted in his defense of Calhoun, it was "the mistaken application of the idea of racial superiority in the defense of slavery" which "had the effect of delaying recognition of the truth in what had been said until the controversy over slavery was at an end."[31] In Merriam's view, Calhoun's theory had been vindicated only after the institution of slavery had been destroyed. With the end of slavery, it had become possible to see the historical and scientific truth that only certain races were capable of self–government.

The historians' admiration of Lincoln, therefore, rested upon what they considered an historic achievement, the establishment of the modern state or nation. Lincoln's own understanding of his actions in defense of constitutionalism was dependent upon the necessity of upholding the conditions of the social compact, which required a reaffirmation of the founding principles of the regime. Yet, the Progressives interpreted his role as an historical vindication of the idea of the state, and the denial of the social compact as the foundation of constitutionalism. Charles Merriam, commenting on what he perceived to be the fundamental accomplishment of Lincoln, observed: "In the new national school, the tendency was to disregard the doctrine of the social contract, and to emphasize strongly the instinctive forces whose action and interaction produces a state. This distinction was developed by Lieber, who held that the great

31. Ibid., 312.

difference between 'people' and 'nation' lies in the fact that the latter possess organic unity...In general, the new school thought of the Union as organic rather than contractual in nature." As Merriam noted, "the contract philosophy was in general disrepute, and the overwhelming tendency was to look upon the nation as an organic product, the result of an evolutionary process."[32]

Merriam concluded, therefore, that it had become necessary to recognize the fact that the concept of the *nation* was dependent upon a theoretical understanding of the state. The notion of a *people*, on the other hand, can only be understood with reference to the theory of a social compact made by individuals. Thus, Merriam insisted that "nation carried with it the idea of an ethnic and geographic unity, constituted without the consent of any one in particular; 'people' was understood to be a body formed by a contract between certain individuals. The very fact that the Union was 'pinned together with bayonets' was enough to show that the doctrine of voluntary consent had faded into the background."[33] In the modern state, it was no longer necessary to establish the legitimacy of government by securing the consent of the governed. Merriam assumed that because the Southern states had not been allowed to secede from the Union, the social compact—like slavery—had become an historical anachronism.

For Merriam, the Civil War itself had destroyed the conditions of the social compact. He concluded from this that

> the general idea was that the United States, by virtue of the community of race, interest, and geographical location, *ought to be* and is a nation; and ought to be held together by force, if no other means would avail. This was the feeling that underlay the great national move-

---

32. Ibid., 297.
33. Ibid., 298.

ment of 1861–1865, and could not fail to be reflected in
the philosophy of that time and in the succeeding interpretations of that event.[34]

History itself had provided the ground of the new theory.
Like evolution, success in the struggle had proved the right-
ness of the cause. Lincoln, who had tried to preserve a regime of civil and religious liberty based on the principles of
the American founding, was celebrated by Progressive social scientists and historians for having established a modern state.

The Southern intellectuals had rejected Lincoln's understanding of the meaning of equality as an abstract truth,
which was the way it had been understood by the American Founders. But, the Northern intellectuals had also rejected Lincoln's defense of the principle of equality. They
insisted that the idea of equality had been undermined by
the discoveries of the new biological and social sciences.
Thus Charles Merriam could argue: "from the standpoint
of modern political science the slave holders were right in
declaring that liberty can be given only to those who have
political capacity enough to use it, and they were also right
in maintaining that two greatly unequal races cannot exist
side by side on terms of perfect equality."[35] Furthermore,
Merriam agreed with the Southerners that "rights do not
belong to men simply as men, but because of the superior
qualities, physical, intellectual, moral or political, which are
characteristic of certain individuals or races."[36] The denial
that the principle of natural human equality was a standard
for political right made it impossible to defend equality as
the fundamental ground of citizenship. The new sciences

---

34. Ibid.
35. Ibid., 250–251.
36. Ibid., 248.

had established race and class as the necessary foundation of political and social life. As a result, equal citizenship based on an understanding of individual natural rights was no longer intelligible as a practical matter.

Nearly all of the scholarly opinion following the Civil War was critical of the North's attempt to establish the former slaves as equal citizens. The North was condemned for extending the franchise, and the South praised for obstructing black voting. The leading political scientist of the day, Columbia's John W. Burgess, observed that "it is the white man's mission, his duty and his right to hold the reins of political power in his own hands...The claim that there is nothing in the color of the skin from the point of view of political ethics is a great sophism. A black skin means membership in a race of men which has never of itself succeeded to reason, has never, therefore created any civilization of any kind."[37] By the end of the nineteenth century the authority of science had come to buttress the claims of historicism. It was as though the theories of Darwin and Hegel had been merged.

It is instructive to see how the historians of the time had come to understand Reconstruction. James Ford Rhodes, "who wrote the first detailed study of the Reconstruction period, fully subscribed to the idea that Negroes were innately inferior and incapable of citizenship...Rhodes thought it a great pity that the North had been unwilling to listen to such men of science as Louis Agassis who could have told them that the Negroes were unqualified for citizenship. 'What the whole country has only learned through years of costly and bitter experience,' declared Rhodes, 'was known to this leader of scientific thought before we ventured on the policy of trying to make negroes intelligent by legislative acts: and

---

37. John William Burgess, *Reconstruction and the Constitution, 1866–1876* (New York: C. Scribner's Sons, 1902), viii–ix, 133.

this knowledge was to be had for the asking by the men who were shaping the policy of the nation."[38] The learned opinion of the time was summed up in a single sentence by William A. Dunning of Columbia University. He noted that "the whole difficulty of Reconstruction...stemmed from the fact that the 'antithesis and antipathy of race and color were crucial and ineradicable'."[39] In looking back on that period, nearly every historian has considered Reconstruction to be a political failure. But, given the intellectual opinion of the time, it is hard to see how it could have succeeded.

IMMIGRATION LAW AND CITIZENSHIP

The importance of race or class for an understanding of immigration and citizenship in the last part of the nineteenth century cannot be overstated. As I have shown above, the concept of race was first understood within the framework of a philosophy of History. In the nineteenth century it came to be understood as a category of science. It was Robert Knox in 1850 who "reintroduced the notion of race into biology,"[40] and the newly formed social sciences were quick to adopt the science of race and eugenics. But with the development of the modern university, the idea of the state also came to be understood on the basis of culture as derivative of the discovery of the historical sense. In the new discipline of political science, John Burgess argued, "the State is the national community, and the government is the

---

38. Thomas F. Gossett, *Race: The History of an Idea in America* (Oxford: Oxford University Press, 1977), 284. Quotes are from James Ford Rhodes, *History of the United States from the Compromise of 1850* (New York: Harper & brothers, 1893, 1906), 7 volumes.
39. W.A. Dunning, *Reconstruction: Political and Economic, 1865–1877* (New York: Harper and Row, 1907), 213.
40. Hannah Augstein, *Race: The Origins of an Idea, 1760–1850* (Bristol: St. Augustine's Press, 1996), xxx.

agent of the State." According to Burgess, "the American state, however, had a longer genealogy and a 'transcendent mission.' It was rooted historically in a 'predominant Teutonic nationality,' and it was destined to be 'the perfection of the Aryan genius for political civilization.' This meant that it was essential neither to 'sectionalize' it into states nor to 'pollute' it with non–Ayran elements."[41]

It was not long before the idea that race was the ground of American citizenship came to dominate the debate concerning immigration. Francis Walker, president of MIT, and former chief of the national census, Daniel Tichenor has observed, "was among the first prominent intellectuals to apply Darwinian and Spencerian theories of racial hierarchy to the new European immigration."[42] Walker was concerned that immigration "was increasingly drawn from the nations of southern and eastern Europe—peoples which have got no great good for themselves out of the race wars of centuries, and out of the unceasing struggle with the hard conditions of nature;...and that have thus far remained hopelessly upon the lowest plane of life."[43] In Walker's view, Darwinian evolutionary theory had provided the best means for determining character and the capacity for citizenship.

In the early 1890s, Walker had "embraced Teutonic theory to justify excluding newer European immigrants. 'They have none of the *inherited instincts and tendencies* which made it comparatively easy to deal with immigration of olden time...They are beaten men from *beaten races*, representing the worst failures in the struggle for existence."[44] Walker is not wrong in suggesting that immigration policy must

---

41. Quoted in John G. Gunnell, *The Descent of Political Theory* (Chicago: University of Chicago Press, 1993), 54.
42. Daniel Tichenor, *Dividing Lines: The Politics of Immigration Control in America*, 78.
43. Francis Walker, "Immigration and Degradation," quoted in ibid.
44. Ibid.

take into account the distinctions between nations in terms of judging the character of prospective citizens. Of course, the American social compact would benefit most from citizens who are likely to value freedom, and presumably they would come from non–despotic and well–governed stable regimes. However, it was not clear that the historical notion of *race*, a new scientific construct in Walker's time which denied that the principle of equality must be understood in terms of nature and natural right, had been responsible for the success of any particular regime.

The new understanding of race was not merely a descriptive account of the differences that exist among men, the result of the variety of regimes, languages, religions, and colors. That kind of knowledge had always been understood in terms of common sense and politics—as friends and enemies, or citizens and strangers. The category of race when linked to science came to be used as a means of distinguishing superior and inferior humans solely by consideration of what had been a new construct—race. Indeed, the new science of eugenics, founded in the 1880s by Francis Galton, cousin of Charles Darwin, had gained popularity as a means of promoting or discouraging population growth by distinguishing between the superior races that ought to produce more offspring, and the inferior races that ought to produce less.

As Jay Varma has observed, it was not long before "the concept that ethnic groups were biologically distinct races entered popular discourse with the institutionalization of the science of eugenics in the early 1900s...which had evolved into the study of racial differences and was defined as the study of agencies under social control that may improve or impair the racial qualities of future generations, either physically or mentally."[45] By the time race had come

---

45. Jay K. Varma, "Eugenics and Immigration Restriction: Lessons for

to be understood as the exclusive consideration for citizenship within the state, its corollary, the unlimited power of government, had become legitimized. The new regulatory power of government offered the possibility of using the science of eugenics not merely for making distinctions among immigrant groups, but also for establishing ranks among citizens as well.

Citizenship, the American Founders had argued, need not be established on the basis of a common faith or common blood. Rather, they believed that a common idea, the belief in the abstract truth that all men are created equal, must provide the only foundation of citizenship. But, once again, with the new authority of science and historicism, there would be a concerted attempt for the next half–century to establish citizenship upon the foundation of race. Consequently, it was the principle of equality that would become the casualty of that transformation in the meaning of citizenship.

Daniel Tichenor has pointed to the change: "drawing inspiration from the new scientific research, Progressive Era restrictionists aimed to build a national regulatory system that excluded immigrants of national and ethnic groups they deemed inferior. Certain that crucial *racial* distinctions existed between Europeans, they yearned for new immigration barriers to guard the nation from the contamination of southern and eastern Europeans."[46]

In the following decades, many authors, including Clinton Stoddard Burr, in *America's Race Heritage,* Madison Grant in *The Passing of the Great Race*, and Charles W. Gould's *America, A Family Matter*, insisted that the white race could be divided into a hierarchy of three races, the

---

Tomorrow," in *Journal of the American Medical Association*, vol. 275, March 6, 1996, 734.
46. Tichenor, *Dividing Lines*, 115.

Mediterranean, Alpine and Nordic. It was the Mediterranean race, primarily Southern and Eastern Europeans, but particularly Russian Jews, who were lowest on the scale, with the Alpines on a somewhat higher level. But, the Nordics were considered the superior race. Indeed, Burr goes so far as to suggest, that "Americanism is actually the racial thought of the Nordic race, evolved after a thousand years of experience."[47] If the European races could be distinguished in such a manner, it was not surprising that the other races were thought to be even further down the scale in terms of intelligence and capacity for self–government.

The first piece of legislation in American history, at the national level, to exclude immigrants on the basis of a scientific understanding of race did not occur until 1882. However, that act did not attempt to exclude Europeans because of race. Rather, the new immigration act resulted in the exclusion of the Chinese, who had become a political problem in California. The Chinese had not been assimilated easily into American society, so the case for exclusion was not difficult to make. But, it was the growing awareness of the importance of race to membership in the new organic state that fueled the demand among many intellectuals and politicians for restricting those who could not be assimilated into society. Daniel Tichenor has observed that "Chinese exclusion called for the federal government to assume unprecedented regulatory authority over immigrant admissions and rights for the explicit purpose of guarding the racial purity of American society. Indeed, most advocates of Chinese exclusion shared a strong 'sense of the state'—one that linked national state–building to the preservation of existing orders of ethnic, racial, and religious hierarchy."[48]

---

47. Quoted in John Higham, *Strangers in the Land*, 273.
48. Tichenor, *Dividing Lines*, 87–88.

The Chinese case is instructive, therefore, because that exclusion was defended on the ground of a new understanding of race and science as decisive for determining capacity for citizenship. It was thought that only those of common blood—whose superiority and thus qualification for membership in the state is determined by science—can be eligible for citizenship. If the state is the manifestation of a moral will, and will becomes intelligible as an embodiment of a people through race, citizenship in the state must be understood to be derived from the fundamental inequality of man as established by the differences among the races.

It is clearly the case that not everyone is entitled to citizenship in America, or any other sovereign nation. Immigrants can be excluded on the basis of race, religion, nationality, illiteracy, or many other reasons. That is because republican governments, unlike despotic regimes, must take into account the character of its potential citizens. Prior to the Civil War, the social compact was understood in terms of the principles of equality and liberty. Thus, as noted above, the problem of immigration was understood in terms of prudence or morality. Throughout the early part of the nineteenth century, there had been considerable political pressure to pass national legislation restricting immigration on the basis of religion, nationality, color, or language. Protestants wanted to restrict Irish Catholics because of their religion. But, they could never persuade the Congress to pass legislation banning immigration on the ground of religious differences. Nonetheless, there were numerous restrictions based on health, disease, mental disability, and character or morals—such as preventing prostitutes and criminals, or those of unsavory character, from becoming citizens.[49]

---

49. Before the Progressive understanding of immigration and citizenship had been established on the ground of race, national and state laws had pursued prudential policies which restricted immigration and citizenship

The 1924 Immigration Act was the culmination of nearly a half–century of effort on behalf of a view that celebrated the rational state as the embodiment of the moral will of a people. That will had come to be defined by blood, race, class, or culture. The scholarship in the defense of racial superiority had been generated in the empirical research of the new social and biological sciences. Many of those social science departments had established their legitimacy within the newly established research universities and the research generated by social science would become important in bolstering the movement to restrict immigration on the basis of race.

The restrictionists had many influential supporters in the elites and the intellectual classes, as well as among labor unions. The labor unions opposed unrestricted immigration because they believed that it had caused a surplus of cheap labor which kept down the wages of native American workers. The intellectuals, on the other hand, were in favor of restricting immigration because they thought it necessary that the economy and society should be brought under state control. In their view, it was the business interests that profited from unlimited immigration. Frank Julian Warne,

---

on moral grounds. In 1882, the national government had tried to simplify the task of making prudential judgments by focusing on race. If race had not been taken into account as decisive, and if a restrictive immigration policy was desirable—as it would come to be in a few years— it would have been necessary to establish immigration policy on other grounds. In that case, immigration and citizenship laws could have restricted those whose morals—using opium, pimping, maintaining allegiance to the Emperor, or a foreign sovereign—were incompatible with the character necessary for good citizenship. Indeed, some states had attempted to pass legislation on similar moral grounds. The fundamental necessity of any immigration policy is that of preserving and perpetuating the social compact of free and equal citizens. It is possible to exclude anyone from immigration into a sovereign country. Indeed, the borders may be closed. But, it is not possible to deny the principle of the regime—equality—without undermining the conditions of the social compact itself.

the former secretary of the New York State Immigration Commission, insisted that mass immigration had made it easier for government to neglect the social and economic welfare of American citizens. Warne maintained that "factory laws, women and children in industry, workingmen's insurance, and widows' pensions...would in all probability have been established...several decades earlier if there had been no European immigration of the magnitude of the past three decades."[50]

In the view of many of the Progressive intellectuals, free immigration had made it possible to ignore the social ills brought about by unrestricted capitalism. As Tichenor has written, "the decentralized, self–regulating society that prevailed for much of American history was, in the view of the Progressive Era restrictionists, a luxury of the past."[51] Joseph Lee, a civic reformer, noted the difference in the meaning of liberty: "In political life, liberty meant until recently the minimum of control necessary to secure equal opportunity...We have begun to realize the control of man over nature, and to see that the highest results come from the collective effort consciously directed to an end. These considerations have a direct bearing upon the question of immigration regulation."[52] In the new view, the responsibility for the social welfare of its members rests solely with the government of the state.

In 1916, the newly established Progressive publication, *The New Republic*, made this clear in an editorial: "Freedom of migration from one country to another appears to be one of the elements of nineteenth century liberalism that is fated to disappear. The responsibility of the state for the

---

50. Quoted in Peter H. Wang, *Legislating Normalcy: The Immigration Act of 1924* (San Francisco: R & E Research Associates, 1975), 2.
51. Tichenor, *Dividing Lines*, 114.
52. Quoted in ibid.

welfare of its individual members is progressively increasing. The democracy of today cannot permit...social ills to be aggravated by excessive immigration."[53] Of course, on practical grounds, every nation, including one based upon a social compact, must limit immigration to prevent social ills, or for many other reasons as well. But, the Progressive rejection of the old liberalism was based upon a repudiation of the social compact in which private individuals and civil and economic associations, and not the state, determined the meaning of freedom and the welfare of individuals.

In addition, many specialists in the social sciences, bolstered by the intelligence testing done in World War I, were quick to interpret the data as evidence for excluding certain races. This debate reached its peak after the Great War. In 1923, Henry Fairfield Osborn spoke enthusiastically about the results of intelligence testing carried out by the Army: "I believe those tests were worth what the war [World War I] cost, even in human life, if they served to show clearly to our people the lack of intelligence in our country, and the degrees of intelligence in different races who are coming to us, in a way which no one can say is the result of prejudice...We have learned once and for all that the negro is not like us."[54] It is clear that social scientists such as Osborn could no longer understand the meaning of equality as a political principle. It was not possible for them to see what it is that men have in common by nature. Therefore, they had come to believe that the differences between blacks and whites were as fundamental politically as those between men and animals.

When Walter Lippmann questioned some of the interpretations of the psychologists, he was ridiculed by many

---

53. Quoted in ibid., 146–147.
54. Quoted in Stephan Jay Gould, *The Mismeasure of Man* (New York: W.W. Norton, 1981), 231.

social scientists, including Lewis Terman, who had published the Stanford–Binet scale of intelligence in 1916. Indeed, Dr. William McDougall, professor of psychology at Harvard, insisted that because of Lippmann's failure to accept the scientific explanation of the testing results, he was "denying also the theory of organic evolution, and he should come out openly on the side of Mr. [William Jennings] Bryan. For the theory of the heredity of mental qualities is a corollary of the theory of organic evolution."[55]

The denial of the principle of equality was stated most openly by Dr. Harry N. Laughlin, eugenics consultant to the House Judiciary Committee on Immigration and Naturalization. He noted "we in this country have been so imbued with the idea of democracy, or the equality of all men, that we have left out of consideration the matter of blood or natural born hereditary mental and moral differences. No man who breeds pedigreed plants and animals can afford to neglect this thing."[56] In the same vein, Prescott Hall, writing in the *Journal of Heredity*, urged a world–wide application of Darwinian principles. Hall contended that "eugenics among individuals is encouraging propagation of the fit, and limiting or preventing the multiplication of the unfit. World eugenics is doing precisely the same thing as to races considered as wholes. Immigration restriction is a species of segregation on a large scale, by which inferior stocks can be prevented from both diluting and supplanting good stock."[57]

Immigration policy in America had gone from one based on an understanding of the natural rights of men to one based on historical and biological science. As Abba Schwartz has noted, "The National Origins provisions of the immigration

---

55. Quoted in Gossett, *Race*, 377.
56. Quoted in Tichenor, *Dividing Lines*, 144.
57. Ibid.

law of 1924 marked the actual turning point from immigration control based on the asylum idea...[to one] definitely in favor of the biological basis."[58] The regime of civil and religious liberty had often provided asylum to those who had been persecuted because of religious belief. Religion, although a problem when allied with despotic governments, had also helped shape the kind of character necessary in a regime which required self-restraint and self-government. The authority of biology had come to determine the most important factor in establishing the capacity for citizenship. It is no small part of the tragedy of the period that by the time Hitler had come to power in the decade of the 1930s, the Immigration Act of 1924 made it nearly impossible for Jews to find an asylum in America.

The problem posed by unrestricted immigration would become a fundamental preoccupation of the nation after the First World War. The Immigration Act of 1924, as a result of national or group quotas, seemed to have legitimized the view that the creation of a racial hierarchy to determine immigration policy was the primary motivation for the legislation. But that perception is not altogether accurate. There were numerous prudential reasons for restricting immigration; racial quotas would become only the most publicized reason for doing so. The War itself had temporarily resolved the problem; very little immigration had been possible during the War. The War had fanned the flames of hostility against foreigners. Not surprisingly, however, because they were the enemy in that War, resentment against the foreign born was directed first against a superior race, the Germans. As Tichenor has noted, "rallies held by the German–American Alliance in support of peace with Germany dismayed the American public in 1915–16, accentuating native fears

---

58. Abba Schwartz, *The Open Society* (New York: Simon & Schuster, 1968), 105–106.

about the loyalties of the country's large foreign–born population."[59]

That fear prompted suspicions about the character and reliability of nearly all foreign born populations. By the end of the War, the Bolshevik Revolution in Russia had complicated the problem of immigration in a way that made it easier to defend restrictions based on race. Americans had begun to fear that a flood of refugees from Eastern Europe would include radicals and communist agitators. The racial theories seemed to support the view that Eastern and Southern Europeans lacked the proper intelligence and character for citizenship. Predictably, after the War, however, the hostility against the Germans would subside. But the racial theories would emerge once again to be used in support of the animus against the Southern and Eastern Europeans. Thus, in the early 1920s, there had been a flood of popular and academic books that decried the mixing of the races. In addition, the eugenics movement would gain an unprecedented respectability, not only in the social sciences, but in the government, the courts, and the public at large.

In the aftermath of the War, there was nearly universal agreement that some restrictions on immigration were necessary. Indeed, there was considerable public support for a ban on all immigration, in which case quotas would have been unnecessary. But, there was little political support for closing the borders. In the absence of unrestricted immigration, it was necessary to determine who should be given preference in terms of immigration into the United States. The Quota Act of 1921, known as the Dillingham Act, was the first to establish immigration quotas based on the country of origin. Immigration would be limited to three percent of each European nationality living in the United States, with

---

59. Tichenor, *Dividing Lines*, 129.

the total number of immigrants restricted to 355,000 per year.[60]

The practical problem of establishing quotas revolved around the necessity of determining an accurate way of distinguishing American citizens and establishing their country of origin. That was not an easy task. As Mae M. Ngai has noted: "The census of 1790, the nation's first, did not include information about national origin or ancestry. The census did not differentiate the foreign–born until 1850 and did not identify the places of birth of parents of the native-born until 1890. Immigration was unrecorded before 1820 and not classified according to origin until 1899, when it was arranged, not by politically defined nation–states, but according to a taxonomy called 'races and peoples'."[61]

It was difficult, therefore, to determine the country of origin for purposes of establishing quotas before the census of 1900. Moreover, many of the immigrants had come into the United States in the last decade of the nineteenth century. The new immigrants wanted the most recent census for the purpose of determining the numbers of each nationality living in the country. In the Dillingham Act, it was decided that the 1910 census would be used to establish that number for purposes of establishing quotas. This decision was not unnecessarily divisive and it appeared that most could live with those restrictions based on that census.

The problem arose when it came time to reauthorize the Dillingham Act. By 1924, the demand for racial quotas had gained momentum in Congress, and particularly in the House. When the Republicans took control of Congress in 1919, Albert Johnson (R-WA) took over the Immigration

---

60. See Tichenor, *Dividing Lines*, 143.
61. Mae M. Ngai, "The Architecture of Race in American Immigration Law: A Reexamination of the Immigration Act of 1924," *The Journal of American History*, vol. 86, issue 1, 71.

Committee. He had a long association with the Immigration Restriction League. Beginning in the 1890s, the IRL had attempted to lobby Congress using social science expertise to buttress the case for immigration restriction. Subsequently, Johnson hired Harry Laughlin to serve as the committee's expert on eugenics. Experts had long argued for "the proper eugenic selection of the incoming alien millions." They insisted that this could be done "not by killing off the less fit, but by preventing them from coming into the State, either by being born into it or by migration."[62] With Johnson in charge, the House committee went to great lengths to limit the quotas of those races thought to be inferior.

The provision of the 1924 Act that caused the greatest outcry was the change that would require that the 1890 census—rather than the 1910 census—be used to determine national quotas. It was based on the assumption that those Americans who had arrived before 1890, largely of the Nordic and Alpine races, were to be preferred to the later immigrants. In terms of actual numbers, the act did not result in significantly reducing the number of immigrants from Southern and Eastern Europe. The restrictions on the total number of immigrants allowed in the Dillingham Act had already done that. The number of new immigrants from Southern and Eastern Europe was very small. The damage that was done resulted from the fact that the new law appeared to establish a rank among citizens that would be based upon racial group characteristics. Moreover, there was no quota for immigrants from the Western hemisphere. Thus, immigrants from Mexico and Latin America were not affected.

Significant elements of both political parties and most elites had supported immigration policies based on racial superiority. But the Republican Party—perhaps because

---

62. Tichenor, *Dividing Lines*, 143

it dominated electoral politics during the 1920s—came to be viewed as the party most responsible for defending a new kind of inequality. Subsequently, the party of Lincoln would have great difficulty in reestablishing itself as the defender of the principle of equality. As a result, many of those constituencies that had supported the Republican Party, including blacks and Jews who had voted in support of the Republicans in the election of 1920, would abandon the Party.

Moreover, the newer immigrants who had come to America after the 1880s settled largely in the big cities and urban areas. They were assimilated by the Democratic Party machines that had dominated politics and elections in those cities. Although most of the ethnic immigrants voted for Democrats in local elections, many of them voted for Republicans nationally, beginning in the 1890s and continuing into the early part of the twentieth century. Indeed, Woodrow Wilson had to repudiate many of his academic writing on race in order to lure some of these new immigrants away from the Republican Party.

By the end of the decade of the 1920s, those immigrants and their children were no longer competitive for the Republican Party, and would not be for nearly a half-century. Ironically, it was Franklin D. Roosevelt's Democratic Party, which was committed to the establishment of a new administrative state that would make its appeal on the basis of equality and equal citizenship. Roosevelt insisted, however, that it was the government of the modern state, and not the principles of the social compact, that would determine the meaning of equality and equal citizenship.

Although many in Congress had worked to mobilize constituencies on the ground of race, there were many others who had argued for immigration restriction in a way that was compatible with an understanding of equality and character, too, as necessary for good citizenship. Although President Harding and Vice President Calvin Coolidge were in favor of immigration restrictions, their rhetoric was far different than that coming out of Congress. Indeed, when Coolidge became President he appeared to handle the problem in a prudential manner. First, Coolidge defended immigration restrictions on the practical ground that "we should have no more aliens to cope with...than our institutions are able to handle."[63] Furthermore, his defense of those restrictions was not intended to polarize the nation by categorizing American citizens in terms of race. Therefore, he insisted that "restrictive immigration is not an offensive but a purely defensive action...We must remember that every object of our institutions of society and government will fail unless America is kept American."[64] America must be understood not in terms of race but in terms of an idea.

The perpetuation of the social compact is, of course, in the hands of all who are a part of it. Therefore, Coolidge was determined to prevent immigrants from any nation who would undermine that compact from becoming American citizens. He maintained that "there is no room in our midst for those whose direct purpose is political, social, or economic mischief, and whose presence jeopardizes the physical or moral health of the community." In the final analysis, Coolidge understood the problem of immigration in the same way as the American Founders, on moral grounds. Therefore, he insisted that "American institutions rest solely on good citizenship and were created by people who had a background of self–government. New arrivals should be limited to our capacity to absorb them into the ranks of good citizenship."[65] Coolidge's rhetoric did not

---

63. Quoted in Wang, *Legislating Normalcy*, 91
64. Ibid., 126.
65. Ibid., 9, 91.

appear to give support to those who would attempt to understand America in terms of class or racial groups.

The Immigration Act of 1965 was defended on the ground that the old national or group criteria, which had established the foundation for the 1924 and 1952 immigration acts, would be replaced by individual criteria. Senator Edward Kennedy noted that "favoritism based on nationality will disappear. Favoritism based on individual worth and qualifications will take its place."[66] President Lyndon Johnson also criticized the national origins quota system because "the ability of new immigrants to come to America depended upon the country of their birth. Only three countries were allowed to supply seventy percent of all the immigrants...This system violated the basic principle of American democracy—the principle that values and rewards each man on the basis of his merit as a man. It has been un-American in the highest sense because it has been untrue to the faith that brought thousands to these shores even before we were a country."[67] Johnson did not say what that faith was.

Both Kennedy and Johnson had denied that immigration policy should be based on nationality or race. Rather, Johnson insisted that the new immigrants should be admitted on the basis of their skills. "Those who can contribute most to this country—to its growth, to its strength, to its spirit—will be the first that are admitted to this land."[68] Kennedy and Johnson may have believed that the neutral category of skill, unrelated to character, is the way in which immigration policy would take into account the capacity of individuals as opposed to groups. But both Kennedy and

---

66. Quoted in Moses Rischin, *Immigration and the American Tradition*, 431.
67. Quoted in ibid., 449.
68. Quoted in ibid.

Johnson were well aware that as citizens of the administrative state, the new immigrants would be important as
members of ethnic and racial groups. Thus, they must have
known that the new immigrants, shaped by the expectations created by government, and not those of a free society,
could become important constituencies for the perpetuation
of the Democratic Party. Moreover, in denying any moral
basis for determining the character of prospective citizens,
they were promoting a policy that would encourage immigrants who would seek benefits from, or become dependent
upon, the administrative state.

The immigrants who came to America after the 1965
Immigration Act, therefore, had fewer reasons to become
citizens of the United States. The administrative state had
begun to expand and consolidate its grip on American politics. Those immigrants who came were often more interested in what the government could provide. It was becoming
less important, therefore, to participate as members of a political community. Although economic opportunity still provided a stimulus for those coming to America, the role of
the federal government had changed in regard to the understanding of the status and rights of immigrants and aliens.
As Daniel Tichenor has observed, "The post–1960s 'rights
revolution' gave immigrants fewer reasons to become citizens. Naturalized voters and parties were no longer the life-
blood of expansive immigration policies."[69]

In the following decades, there is no question that Mexicans and other Latin American immigrants naturalized at
very low rates compared to the earlier periods. Why did this
happen? As Peter Schuck and Rogers Smith have observed:

> The law...increasingly speaks of individual "rights," the
> language of entitlement, rather than of their "interests,"
> the language of policy and accommodation. Moreover, the

---

69. Tichenor, *Dividing Lines,* 220.

> law increasingly emphasizes the values of equality, group interest, and nondiscrimination....And it is welfare state membership, not citizenship that increasingly counts. Political membership uniquely confers little more than the right to vote and the right to remain here permanently; the former is used by only a bare majority of eligible voters, while the latter, although undeniably valuable, is problematic for only a minority of legal aliens.[70]

Moreover, the 1965 act, when interpreted by the bureaucracy and courts, had created a new category of those who could become beneficiaries of government and constituencies of the administrative state—aliens, legal and illegal. As a result of those policies of the bureaucratic apparatus of the state, which blurred the distinction between entitlements and responsibilities, it had become difficult to distinguish between the rights and duties of citizens and non–citizens. With the consolidation of the administrative state, it is difficult to understand the policies of government in any way other than the conferring of benefits to various groups or constituencies without regard for a public good.

The legislative and judicial remedies of the last half-century designed to deal with the problems of immigration and citizenship have not succeeded in lessening the conflict over the protection of fundamental rights. That is because citizenship is still understood in terms of those historical categories of race and class established in the notion of the state. It is not surprising that this failure to understand citizenship as a social compact of the people, based on the principle of equality, has resulted in undermining the distinction between citizens and aliens, legal and illegal. The apparatus of the administrative state has extended rights and privileges to non–citizens that would be incomprehensible

---

70. Peter Schuck and Rogers Smith, *Citizenship Without Consent* (New Haven: Yale University Press, 1995), 106–108.

were it not for the fact that the state, and not the *people*, has become sovereign. As a result, the government of the administrative state has produced an immigration policy which has generated very little public support among American citizens.

Furthermore, the remedies for protecting the civil rights of every American have not united but divided the country. In the public debate on immigration reform there was an explicit linkage between civil rights and immigration reform. As Vice President Hubert Humphrey noted: "We have removed all elements of second–class citizenship from our laws by the Civil Rights Act...We must in 1965 remove all elements in our immigration law which suggests that there are second–class people...We want to bring our immigration law into line with the spirit of the Civil Rights Act of 1964."[71] Not surprisingly, the Civil Rights Act and the Immigration Act of 1965 were primarily justified by their intention to reverse the racism in a society which had sanctioned segregation, and the quotas of the Immigration Act of 1924. But, the remedies for both problems were achieved, not by denying that group status or race ought to be the ground of civil rights or citizenship, but by giving preference to the previously excluded groups and races. In short, it had not been possible to reestablish civil rights, or immigration policy, on the ground of the equality of all individuals.

CONCLUSION

The pervasiveness of an understanding of man and citizenship in terms of race and class has persisted unabated in the past half–century, despite the collapse of Nazism and Communism. In abandoning nature as the standard for political life, the thinkers of the late nineteenth century had turned

---

71. Tichenor, *Dividing Lines*, 215.

to race or class as the means of providing an explanation for the historical differences among men and their differing achievements. Furthermore, the newly created social sciences, with the authority of history and biology behind them, were uniform in their insistence that race should become the foundation for the determination of citizenship. However much racial theories came to be discredited in the twentieth century the theoretical ground, the philosophy of History, upon which the defense of race and class had been established, was never discredited or abandoned.

As a result, it has not been possible to reestablish the protection of the equal rights of citizenship on the ground of an understanding of the principle of equality—as an abstract truth derived from nature. It was that understanding of natural right that had been abandoned as the foundation of citizenship by the Progressives. Thus, it has become clear in light of what occurred in the wake of the passage of the Civil Rights Act of 1964 and the Immigration Act of 1965 that the rights and duties of citizenship, and their enforcement in the courts and bureaucracies, could only be understood on the basis of the Progressive understanding of history and the acceptance of the moral authority of the administrative state.

In practice, therefore, the policies promulgated in the bureaucracies and courts relating to the rights of citizenship have become meaningful only with reference to the state, or group identity. And, groups can be understood in an intelligible way only through the categories derived from race, class, ethnicity, or gender. The result was not a return to the principle of equality—of individual rights but a new kind of group equality which would seek to reverse the old hierarchies (white—or male—dominance, economic class privilege, or racial preference).

Furthermore, when politicians attempt to make prudential arguments concerning immigration policy or civil rights policy on the basis of individual rights—which run counter to the contemporary historicist meaning of group rights—they are considered racist. It becomes impossible in a practical way, therefore, to defend the equal rights of all individuals without reference to race or social status. Ironically, the political defense of the equal rights of individuals, a genuinely non-racist position, becomes vulnerable to the charge of racism precisely because it does not take race, class, or social status, into account. It is not surprising, therefore, that politicians are unwilling or unable to make a compelling defense of the equal rights of individual citizens.

There is a deeper reason for the failure to reestablish the ground of citizenship on the principle of equality as the foundation of the social compact. Such a defense would require an understanding of natural right. But, the modern State itself, and the problems of immigration and citizenship have been understood only in terms of a philosophy of History. In the final analysis, perhaps, Hannah Arendt was right when she insisted, speaking about race and class, that "free public opinion has adopted them to such an extent that not only intellectuals but great masses of people will no longer accept any presentation of past or present facts that is not in agreement with these views."[72] In the absence of an understanding of natural right, history may be intelligible only on the ground of race or class, or some similar variation of historical consciousness derived from the Progressive understanding of the meaning of freedom.

---

72. Hannah Arendt, "Race-Thinking Before Racism," 39.

ABOUT THE AUTHORS

Edward J. Erler is Professor of Political Science at California State University, San Bernardino and a Senior Fellow at the Claremont Institute.

John Marini is Associate Professor of Political Science at University of Nevada, Reno and a Senior Fellow at the Claremont Institute.

Thomas G. West is Professor of Politics at the University of Dallas and a Senior Fellow at the Claremont Institute.

ABOUT THE CLAREMONT INSTITUTE

The Claremont Institute for the Study of Statesmanship and Political Philosophy was founded in 1979 to restore the principles of the American Founding to their rightful, preeminent authority in our national life. The Institute publishes the quarterly *Claremont Review of Books*, sponsors several educational fellowships in the American Founding and conducts a variety of programs that apply the principles of the Founding to the critical public policy issues of our day. Our scholarship extends from strategic to literary studies, from Plato and Aristotle to John Locke and Thomas Jefferson—in short, to all those subjects upon which citizens must draw to preserve and perfect their liberty.

The Claremont Institute
937 West Foothill Blvd.
Claremont, CA 91711
909-621-6825
www.claremont.org